Weaving It Together

Connecting Reading and Writing

MILADA BROUKAL

THOMSON
™
HEINLE

Australia • Canada • Mexico • Singapore • United Kingdom • United States

THOMSON

™

HEINLE

**Weaving It Together: Connecting Reading and Writing,
Book 4/Second Edition**
Milada Broukal

Publisher, Adult and Academic ESL: James W. Brown
Senior Acquisitions Editor: Sherrise Roehr
Sr. Developmental Editor: Ingrid Wisniewska
Sr. Production Editor: Maryellen Killeen
Sr. Marketing Manager: Charlotte Sturdy
Sr. Print Buyer: Mary Beth Hennebury
Editorial Assistant: Audra Longert
Contributing Writer (Video Activities): Barbara Gaffney

Project Manager: Lifland et al., Bookmakers
Compositor: Parkwood Composition
Photography Manager: Sheri Blaney
Photo Researcher: Susan Van Etten
Illustrator: Ashley Van Etten
Cover Designer: Rotunda Design/Gina Petti
Interior Designer: Carole Rollins
Printer: Quebecor World

5 6 7 8 9 10 07 06

For more information contact Heinle, 25 Thomson Place, Boston, Massachusetts 02210 USA, or you can visit our Internet site at http://www.heinle.com

For permission to use material from this text or product contact us:
Tel 1-800-730-2214
Fax 1-800-730-2215
Web www.thomsonrights.com

Library of Congress Cataloging-in-Publication Data

Broukal, Milada.
    Weaving it together: connecting reading and writing/Milada Broukal.
        p. cm.
    Includes bibliographical references.
    Contents: Bk. 4. High intermediate level
    ISBN 0-8384-4831-3
    1. English language—Textbooks for foreign speakers. I. Title.

PE1128 .B7154 2003
428.2'4—dc21   2002032930

Photo credits: Cover: (top) Bonnie Kamin/Index Stock Imagery; (bottom) Carl Rosenstein/Index Stock Imagery. p. 1: © CNAC/MNAM/Dist Réunion des Musees Nationaux/Art Resource, NY. p. 2: (top) © 2003 The Georgia O'Keeffe Foundation/Artists Rights Society (ARS), New York, © Francis Mayer/CORBIS; (center) © 2003 Artists Rights Society (ARS), New York/ADAGP, Paris, Erich Lessing/Art Resource, NY, Musée D'Orsay, Paris, France; (bottom) Erich Lessing/Art Resource, NY, National Gallery, London, Great Britain. p. 3: (top) © 2003 Salvador Dali, Gala-Salvador Dali Foundation/Artists Rights Society (ARS), New York. © Bettmann/CORBIS; (bottom) Erich Lessing/Art Resource, NY, Kunstmuseum, Basel, Switzerland. p. 13: © Jeremy Gardiner. p. 33: © Archivo Iconografico, S.A./CORBIS. p. 45: (top) © Heinle IRB; (bottom) © Comstock. p. 62: © Hulton-Deutsch Collection/CORBIS. p. 73: © Royalty-Free/CORBIS. p. 91: © AFP/CORBIS. p. 102: © CORBIS. p. 117: © Hemera Photo Objects. p. 146: © Gilbert Patrick/CORBIS SYGMA. p. 147: (top row, left to right) © John Burke/Index Stock Imagery; © Jon Riley/Index Stock Imagery; © Steve Dunwell/Index Stock Imagery; (bottom row, left to right) © Ronnie Kaufman/CORBIS; © Left Lane Productions/CORBIS; © Jim McGuire/Index Stock Imagery. p. 158: (left) © Christie's Images/CORBIS; (right) © Hemera Photo Objects. p. 189: © Joe Baraban Photography, Inc./CORBIS. p. 209: © Mary Ann McDonald/CORBIS. p. 210: (top left) © Michael Yamashita/CORBIS; (top right) © Grochowiak Eva/CORBIS SYGMA; (bottom left) © Jim Craigmyle/CORBIS; (bottom right) © Little Blue Wolf Productions/CORBIS. p. 217: © George Lepp/CORBIS. p. 234: © John Nordell/Index Stock Imagery. p. 243: © Bonnie Kamin/Index Stock Imagery.

(continued on page 276)

Brief Contents

Weaving It Together 4 Contents

To the Teacher

Rationale

Weaving It Together, Book 4, is the fourth in a four-book series that integrates reading and writing skills for students of English as a second or foreign language. The complete program includes the following:

Book 1—Beginning Level

Book 2—High Beginning Level

Book 3—Intermediate Level

Book 4—High Intermediate Level

The central premise of *Weaving It Together* is that reading and writing are interwoven and inextricable skills. Good readers write well; good writers read well. With this premise in mind, *Weaving It Together* has been developed to meet the following objectives:

1. To combine reading and writing through a comprehensive, systematic, and engaging process designed to integrate the two effectively.
2. To provide academically bound students with serious and engaging multicultural content.
3. To promote individualized and cooperative learning within moderate-to large-sized classes.

Over the past few years, a number of noted researchers in the field of second language acquisition have written about the serious need to integrate reading and writing instruction in both classroom practice and materials development. *Weaving It Together* is, in many ways, a response to this need.

Barbara Kroll (1993), for example, talks of teaching students to read like writers and write like readers. She notes: "It is only when a writer is able to cast himself or herself in the role of a reader of the text under preparation that he or she is able to anticipate the reader's needs by writing into the text what he or she expects or wants the reader to take out from the text." Through its systematic approach to integrating reading and writing, *Weaving It Together* teaches ESL and EFL students to understand the kinds of interconnections that they need to make between reading and writing in order to achieve academic success.

Linda Lonon Blanton's research (1992) focuses on the need for second language students to develop authority, conviction, and certainty in their writing. She believes that students develop strong writing skills in concert with good reading skills. Blanton writes: "My experience tells me that empowerment, or achieving this certainty and authority, can be achieved only through performance—through the act of speaking and writing about texts, through developing individual responses to texts." For Blanton, as for Kroll and others, both reading and writing must be treated as composing processes. Effective writing instruction must be integrally linked with effective reading instruction. This notion is at the heart of *Weaving It Together.*

Organization of the Text

Weaving It Together, Book 4, contains nine chapters, each of which includes two thematically related readings and addresses a particular aspect of essay organization. At the end of the book, in the Resources for Writers section, there are useful tips on generating ideas, drafting, revising, editing, paraphrasing, summarizing, and quoting.

Each chapter contains the following sequence of activities:

1. **Pre-reading questions and activity:** Each chapter is introduced with a picture, accompanied by a set of discussion questions. This is followed by an activity related to the theme of the chapter. The purpose of the pre-reading questions and activity is to prepare students for the reading by activating their background knowledge and encouraging them to call on and share their experiences.

2. **Readings:** Each chapter contains two high-interest passages related to the theme of the chapter. The second reading is from a book or magazine article. The final chapter includes two readings from works by contemporary authors. Each reading is followed by vocabulary activities, comprehension exercises, and discussion questions.

3. **Vocabulary:** There are two types of vocabulary exercises. The first type uses a multiple-choice format to help students recognize the meaning of new words in context. The second type helps students extend their vocabulary skills to new contexts by, for example, learning to recognize collocations, synonyms, or antonyms.

4. **Comprehension:** There are three types of comprehension exercises. The first, *Looking for Main Ideas,* concentrates on a general understanding of the reading. This exercise may be done after a first reading or used as a pre-reading activity. The second comprehension exercise, *Skimming and Scanning for Details,* concentrates on developing skimming and scanning skills. The third comprehension

exercise, *Making Inferences and Drawing Conclusions,* develops the skill of inferring what is not directly stated in the reading.

5. **Discussion:** Working in small or large groups, students are encouraged to interact with one another to discuss questions that arise from the reading. The discussion questions ask students to relate their experiences to what they have learned from the reading.

6. **Writing a summary, paraphrasing, and research:** These optional writing activities, cross-referenced to the Resources for Writers section, give students practice in specific composition-related skills that are useful for academic study.

7. **Model essay:** Each chapter contains an essay written by an international student whose writing skills are slightly more advanced than those of the writers who will use *Weaving It Together, Book 4.* The essay follows the general rhetorical form of North American academic prose and provides natural preparation for the more specific points taught in the organizing section. Follow-up work and questions about the student essay reinforce essay organization techniques.

8. **Organizing:** In each of the nine chapters, a different aspect of essay writing is developed. These aspects include essay organization, structure, transitions, and rhetorical devices the students may use to develop their own essays. Exercises following the instructional text reinforce the organizational techniques introduced.

9. **Writing practice:** Three different idea-generating techniques are presented on pages 258–260. Before students begin writing their outline, you may want to refer them to these pages to try out and practice a variety of techniques that will help them to activate their background knowledge. Using the ideas they have generated in the pre-writing stage, students next put together an outline for their writing. This outline acts as a framework for the work ahead. The next step is to write a rough draft of the essay. *Weaving It Together* encourages students to write several drafts, since writing is an ongoing process. Students can then work on their own or with a partner to check their essays, making any necessary alterations. Teachers are encouraged to add to the checklist provided any further points they consider important. Next, students are encouraged to work with a partner or their teacher to correct spelling, punctuation, vocabulary, and grammar. Finally, students prepare the final version of the essay.

Optional Expansion Activities

1. **Video activity:** At the end of each chapter is a video activity related to the CNN videotapes that accompany this series. The video activity can be used to expand vocabulary and themes in the chapter. Each video activity ends with a writing or discussion question, which can be used as a springboard for further writing.

2. **Internet activity:** Following the video activity is an Internet activity, which gives students the opportunity to develop their Internet research skills. This activity may be done in a classroom setting, under the guidance of the teacher, or—if students have Internet access—as a homework task leading to a classroom presentation or discussion. Each Internet activity has two parts. The first part involves doing some research on the Internet using the key words suggested. The second part involves evaluating web sites in order to assess the reliability of the information they contain.

Journal Writing

In addition to doing the projects and exercises in the book, I strongly recommend that students be instructed to keep a journal in which they correspond with you. The purpose of this journal is for them to tell you how they feel about the class each day. It gives them an opportunity to tell you what they like, what they dislike, what they understand, and what they don't understand. By having students explain what they have learned in the class, you can discover whether they understand the concepts taught.

Journal writing is effective for two major reasons. First, because this type of writing focuses on fluency and personal expression, students always have something to write about. Second, journal writing can be used to identify language concerns and trouble spots that need further review. In its finest form, journal writing becomes an active dialogue between teacher and student that permits you to learn more about your students' lives and to individualize their language instruction.

References

Blanton, Linda Lonon. 1992. "Reading, Writing, and Authority: Issues in Developmental ESL." *College ESL*, 2, 11–19.

Kroll, Barbara. 1993. "Teaching Writing *Is* Teaching Reading: Training the New Teacher of ESL Composition." In *Reading in the Composition Classroom*. Boston: Heinle & Heinle Publishers, pp. 61–81.

To the Student

This book will teach you to read and write in English. You will study readings on selected themes and learn strategies for writing good essays on those themes. In the process, you will be exposed to the writings and ideas of others, as well as to ways of expressing your own ideas so that you can work toward writing an essay of four or five paragraphs in good English.

It is important for you to know that writing well in English may be quite different from writing well in your native language. Good Chinese, Arabic, or Spanish writing is different from good English writing. Not only are the styles different, but the organization is different too.

The processes of reading and writing are closely interconnected. Therefore, in this book, we are weaving reading and writing together. I hope that the readings in the book will stimulate your interest to write and that *Weaving It Together* will make writing in English much easier for you.

Note for the New Edition

In this new edition of *Weaving It Together, Book 4*, I have added new vocabulary exercises to extend your vocabulary practice. There is a new chapter on the topic of issues for debate and a new chapter with readings from literature. For those of you who enjoy using different media, I have also added CNN video and Internet activities. I hope that you will enjoy using these new features and that *Weaving It Together* will continue to help you toward success.

CHAPTER ONE

Artists

Pre-Reading Questions

Discuss these questions.

1. Most of Frida Kahlo's works are portraits of herself. What do you think this tells us about her?

2. Which other famous artists painted self-portraits? What do the portraits say about their lives and feelings?

3. Describe the life of an artist you know. Do you think it is difficult to be an artist? Do artists have to face hardships that other working people don't?

Activity

Match the name of each artist with the facts about his or her life. Then say which artist is your favorite and why.

Salvador Dali   Vincent van Gogh   Claude Monet
Georgia O'Keeffe   Paul Gauguin

1. This artist studied art in Chicago and New York and then became a teacher. He/she went back to being a painter in 1918. In 1924, this artist married a photographer. He/she loved the New Mexico desert so much that he/she went to live there in 1929. This artist painted dramatic abstract landscapes, flowers, and other objects of nature. He/she was known for his/her independent lifestyle.

2. This artist was born in Paris and studied art there. While in Paris, he/she met other future impressionists like himself/herself. After a period of poverty in the 1870s, he/she became more financially secure. He/she then moved to a town in France called Giverny and painted works in series, such as *Rouen Cathedral* and *Waterlilies*.

3. This artist is considered a tragic painter because he/she never achieved recognition in his/her lifetime. In 1888, he/she moved from Paris to Arles in the south of France. Gauguin visited him/her there, and the two had violent disagreements, which may have led to his/her first mental seizure. He/she started to express his/her emotional state in his/her work. In 1890, this artist moved north to Auver-sur-Oise, where he/she committed suicide.

4. This artist is one of the most famous surrealist artists. This artist was only six when he/she sold his/her first painting. By the time this artist reached the age of 75, he/she was so famous that a letter would reach him/her addressed only with the word *España* (Spain, which was his/her native country) and the sketch of a moustache. His/her works are highly realistic in style and have a strange dreamlike imagery.

5. In 1883, this artist gave up his/her job as a stockbroker and became a full-time painter. He/she left his/her spouse and children and emigrated from Paris to Tahiti. He/she was attracted to Polynesia because he/she believed primitive art and life were superior to so-called civilization. He/she painted the life of the people of the islands. Although this artist became less happy with life in Tahiti, he/she remained there until his/her death.

Independence, rebelliousness, self-assurance—these are traits shared by many famous people. They are found particularly among artists, and certainly in Frida Kahlo, who belonged to the first generation of famous North American women artists.

Even as a child, Mexico's best-known woman painter exhibited an independent, rebellious spirit and lack of restraint that often got her into trouble. She preferred to run, jump, and skip instead of walk, and she found it difficult to control herself even in church, where she giggled and teased her younger sister.

At the age of six, however, Frida's life changed dramatically. She got polio and was confined to her bed for nine months. The disease left Frida's right leg shorter and thinner than her left, and when she had recovered enough to return to school, she walked with a limp. She was often teased by her playmates, and although that was emotionally painful for her, she compensated by being outgoing and gained a reputation as a "character." Her father encouraged her to play sports to strengthen her leg, and eventually she was able to walk quite well. Frida's father, Guillermo, a professional photographer and amateur painter, was a great influence in her life.

In 1922, at the age of 15, Frida was enrolled at the National Preparatory School in Mexico City, which was near her hometown of Coyoacan. This was the beginning of the postrevolutionary period in Mexico, and the country was experiencing a time of cultural rebirth as well as reform. There was a strong spirit of nationalism and pride in Mexico's heritage. Frida identified with the revolution intellectually, emotionally, and spiritually.

After a few months at the school, Frida adopted a radical[1] new look. Although her father, whom she adored, was European, Frida rejected her European clothes in favor of overalls.[2] She cut her thick, black hair short like a boy's and rode around Coyoacan on a bicycle—

---

[1]radical = completely different.

[2]overalls = loose pants fastened over the shoulders, usually worn by workers over other clothes.

shocking everyone. She even changed her birthdate from 1907 to 1910 to show her sympathy with the Mexican Revolution and to identify herself with the beginnings of modern Mexico.

Frida thrived on[3] intellectual, social, and cultural stimulation at school. She made friends easily and quickly became part of the notorious Cachuchas, a group of seven boys and two girls—intelligent yet rebellious students who named themselves after the caps worn at the school. Their keen[4] minds were matched only by their contempt for authority and capacity for trouble. Frida's natural independence and mischievous[5] nature fit right in. She cut classes and joined in their escapades.[6]

One day, the Cachuchas let a donkey loose in a classroom. Another time, one of the Cachuchas set off fireworks next to a dog, who ran wildly through the school, creating chaos. Frida was even expelled from school once but managed to regain entrance by boldly appealing to the minister of education.

Meanwhile Frida was developing a strong sense of self-assurance and belief in herself. She showed an aptitude for science and intended to go on to medical school and become a doctor. Although she didn't become a physician, her studies in biology and physiology later influenced her work. In many of her paintings, hearts, glands, and other organs are displayed, both inside and outside the body.

A turning point[7] occurred in Frida's life in September 1925, when she was involved in a near-fatal accident. The bus in which she was riding home after school collided with a trolley car. The impact caused a metal rail to break loose, piercing Frida's entire body with the steel rod. The Red Cross doctors who arrived and examined the victims separated the injured from the dying, giving the injured first priority. They took one look at Frida and put her with the hopeless cases.

The doctors eventually treated Frida, and miraculously she survived. She suffered a broken spine, collarbone, and pelvis and two broken ribs. Her right leg was broken in eleven places, and her right foot was crushed. Her left shoulder was dislocated. From that point on, Frida Kahlo would never live a day without pain.

---

[3]thrived on = grew vigorously or developed successfully with.

[4]keen = sharp, quick at understanding.

[5]mischievous = likely to cause trouble.

[6]escapades = wild or exciting acts, usually causing trouble.

[7]turning point = a time of important change.

Although Frida recovered enough to lead a fairly normal life, the accident had severe psychological and physical consequences. She had to abandon her plans to become a doctor, and she had to recognize that she would be a near-invalid for the rest of her life. Her slowly healing body kept her in bed for months, and it was during this time that Frida began to paint. She read every book on art she could get her hands on. Exactly one year after her accident, she produced her first painting, a self-portrait dedicated to[8] her school boyfriend, the leader of the Cachuchas.

Some artists look to nature or society for their inspiration, but Frida Kahlo looked inward. After her crippling accident, Frida depicted her pain in haunting,[9] dreamlike self-portraits. Most of her 200 paintings explore her vision of herself. In *The Broken Column* (1944), her body is open to reveal a cracked column in place of her spine. In *The Wounded Deer* (1946), a small deer with Frida's head and a body pierced with arrows runs through the woods.

In 1929, Frida married the celebrated Mexican artist Diego Rivera. It would be an emotionally turbulent marriage, however, with a divorce in 1939 and remarriage in 1940. Diego made no secret of his infidelities and caused Frida much pain, although his devotion and admiration for her as an artist never diminished. Diego's betrayal of Frida's devotion inflicted great injury on her, as is revealed in a series of paintings depicting their relationship. "I have suffered two accidents in my life," she wrote, "one in which a streetcar ran over me. The other is Diego."

Frida's condition required many operations to try to straighten her spine and repair her foot, but with each one, her condition seemed to worsen. Often she painted in bed with an easel[10] her mother had designed for her. Her health seriously declined when she was in her forties, but Frida always kept her lively spirit. By then she was internationally known. When a Mexican gallery wanted to have a major exhibition of her work, she arranged to have her elaborately decorated, four-poster bed[11] carried into the gallery so that she could receive people.

---

[8]dedicated to = made as a tribute to.

[9]haunting = not easily forgotten, remaining in the mind.

[10]easel = a wooden frame that holds a canvas while it is being painted.

[11]four-poster bed = a bed with four corner posts designed to support curtains.

Frida died in July 1954, in the same room of the bright blue house in which she had been born. She left her work as her legacy,[12] to be sure. But equally inspirational is her life story—and the fact that, by transforming pain into brilliant art, Frida Kahlo triumphed[13] over misfortune.

---

[12]legacy = something received by others after a person's death.
[13]triumphed = was victorious or succeeded.

Vocabulary

Select the letter of the answer that is closest in meaning to the italicized word or phrase.

1. Independence, rebelliousness, *self-assurance*—these are traits shared by many famous people.
   a. optimism
   b. confidence
   c. strength
   d. moodiness

2. Kahlo showed a lack of *restraint* that often got her into trouble.
   a. stress
   b. force
   c. self-control
   d. laziness

3. In church, she giggled and *teased* her sister.
   a. made fun of
   b. encouraged
   c. punched
   d. punished

4. Although she was often teased by her playmates, and this was emotionally painful for her, she *compensated* by being outgoing.
   a. rewarded herself
   b. made up for it
   c. forgave them
   d. attacked them

5. Kahlo became part of the *notorious* Cachuchas, a group of seven boys and two girls—intelligent yet rebellious students who named themselves after the caps worn at the school.
   a. unpopular
   b. fearless
   c. disreputable
   d. unequaled

6. The Cachuchas' keen minds were matched only by their *contempt for* authority and capacity for trouble.
   a. doubt of
   b. devotion to
   c. envy of
   d. hatred of

7. The *impact* of the bus colliding with the trolley car caused a metal rail to break loose.
   a. crash
   b. disaster
   c. conflict
   d. noise

8. In September 1925, Kahlo was involved in a near-*fatal* accident.
   a. dangerous
   b. alarming
   c. unavoidable
   d. deadly

9. After her accident, Kahlo *depicted* her pain in self-portraits.
   a. advertised
   b. taught
   c. portrayed
   d. determined

10. Kahlo's marriage to Diego Rivera was emotionally *turbulent.*
    a. stormy
    b. romantic
    c. strong
    d. delicate

Vocabulary Extension

Part A

Match the adjectives with the nouns as they were used in the context of the reading. Look back at the reading to check your answers. Add two more nouns that may be used with each adjective.

   a. artist
   b. decoration
   c. look
   d. group
   e. accident
   f. turbulence

1. _c_ radical   look   _____   _____

2. ___ notorious   _____   _____   _____

3. ___ fatal   _____   _____   _____

4. ____ celebrated   _____   _____   _____

5. ____ emotional   _____   _____   _____

6. ____ elaborate   _____   _____   _____

Part B

Make questions about Frida Kahlo's life, using each of the word combinations in Part A.

Example:

In what way did Frida have a *radical look?*

With a partner, take turns asking and answering your questions.

Comprehension

Looking for the Main Ideas

Write complete answers to the following questions.

1. What is the main idea of paragraph 3?

2. What is paragraph 9 mostly about?

3. Which line states the main idea of paragraph 11?

4. Which sentences contain the main idea of paragraph 12?

Skimming and Scanning for Details

Scan the reading quickly to find the answers to these questions. Circle the letter of the best answer.

1. As a young girl, Frida Kahlo was _____.
   a. sweet-natured   c. lazy
   b. studious   d. rebellious

2. Polio left Kahlo with a limp, and as a result she became _____.
   a. shy and withdrawn   c. polite and graceful
   b. outgoing and unconventional   d. unfriendly and mean

3. Kahlo's father was a _____.
   a. photographer
   b. politician
   c. psychologist
   d. professor

4. At school, Kahlo joined _____.
   a. the revolution
   b. the debating team
   c. a group of rebellious students
   d. an art club

5. When Kahlo was in school, her goal was to become _____.
   a. an artist
   b. a scientist
   c. a doctor
   d. a revolutionary soldier

6. Which area of study eventually influenced Kahlo's painting?
   a. math
   b. physiology
   c. history
   d. literature

7. Kahlo began to paint _____.
   a. while she was a member of the Cachuchas
   b. after an accident left her bedridden
   c. during the Mexican Revolution
   d. when she was still a child

8. Which of the following does *not* describe Kahlo's artwork?
   a. She painted many beautiful landscapes.
   b. She often used herself as a subject for her work.
   c. She painted pictures showing pain and suffering.
   d. She painted even when she was very ill.

9. Kahlo considered her marriage to Diego Rivera _____.
   a. a convenient arrangement
   b. one of the best things that ever happened to her
   c. essential to the advancement of her career
   d. a painful aspect of her life

10. At the time of her death, Kahlo was _____.
   a. still an unknown artist
   b. not accepted as an accomplished artist
   c. sorry she had ever taken up art
   d. a famous North American woman artist

Making Inferences and Drawing Conclusions

Some of the following statements can be inferred from the reading, and others cannot. Circle the number of each statement that can be inferred.

1. Shy, withdrawn people are not likely to achieve fame as bold, confident people.

2. Sometimes tragic incidents can turn out to be positive influences in our lives.

3. Frida Kahlo was influenced by events that occurred both to her and in the outside world.

4. Kahlo was easily intimidated by those in positions of authority.

5. Several events in Kahlo's life prove that she had a weak character.

6. If it were not for the bus accident in which Kahlo was involved, she probably would never have become a famous artist.

7. Kahlo used her art as a means to express her personal feelings.

8. Kahlo's painting can be described as cheerful and optimistic.

9. Kahlo's marriage to Diego Rivera influenced her art.

10. Kahlo's physical disabilities would have eventually led her to withdraw from society.

Discussion

Discuss these questions with your classmates.

1. How do you think that painting helped Frida Kahlo with her problems?

2. Many of Kahlo's paintings express pain and tragedy. Do you like to see this in a work of art? If so, why? If not, what would you like to see?

3. Many people judge a work of art by how realistic it is and by the technical skill of the artist. They may look at a piece of modern art and say, "Anyone can do that." Is evidence of an original mind also important? Discuss.

4. Is it important to know about an artist's life in order to understand his or her work?

Digital Photo Illustration

The following passage is from the introduction to the book Digital Photo Illustration *by Jeremy Gardiner, professor of Digital Arts at the London College of Music and Media. This book was published by Van Nostrand Reinhold in 1994.*

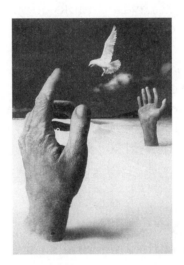

Painting has reclaimed the territory it lost in 1839 when the invention of photography made Paul Delaroche declare "From today painting is dead." Today the marriage of electronic paint systems and digital photography is bridging the gap between painting and photography. In the last ten years digital images have turned the history of imagemaking on its head by making a photograph as plastic and changeable as painting.

The history of photography has always followed the path of technological developments. When photogravure[1] was introduced in the middle of the nineteenth century it enabled periodicals and books to use pictures. Then push button cameras and fast printing papers made the technology available to everyone. Industrial and commercial applications have even influenced the size and shape of photographs.

[1]photogravure = a process in which prints are made by photographic methods.

Business and industry today also drive the evolution of new technology; as prices of software and hardware drop and performance, user interface, and output get better, the old preconceived boundaries between art and technology will fade away.

Conventional photography is a linear process that involves exposure, development, and printing. Digital images have specific advantages over material ones. They can be transmitted, manipulated, and stored easily. . . .

Photography has never told the truth anyway—it has always been the photographer who framed the picture and chose the viewpoint. This is an evolutionary[2] process not a revolutionary one. Artists and photographers have been collaging, . . . retouching, . . . for over a hundred years. Many definable qualities of digital photo illustration were anticipated by artists. Photomontage[3] emerged in the nineteenth century and became a powerful tool in the hands of artists like Heartfield, Rodchenko, and Moholy Nagy.

[Today] two generations of artists and designers have soaked in the glare of television. Images on a screen form our knowledge of the world today. As a result much digital photo illustration presents us with work that is conceptual and secondhand, and like many images from the mass media this genre already has a powerful hold on human perceptions.

Working with a computer enables the individual to interact with the raw material of our culture directly. Digital photo illustration is an attempt to secure the freedom of artistic expression in an effort to overcome what is in danger of becoming an everyday electronic style.

All image processing systems are founded on the same idea. Any picture, whether it is a drawing, a painting, or a photograph, can be turned into the binary[4] data understood by a computer. With enough computer power this data can be manipulated easily. It is obvious that all graphic production is quickly becoming part of a big electronic chain. When artists put down their pencils and storyboards and begin working with the computer, physical production will no longer be managed by production craftspeople. The physical production process will have begun the moment the image is created. However, digital image processing still remains a post-creative production process. Even

---

[2]evolutionary = gradually developing.

[3]photomontage = a picture made by combining several pictures.

[4]binary = having two parts.

though the computer opens up a wealth of creative potential, few people have come to grips with approaching it in this way. Digital photo illustration looks at the processes and methods that can be used to exploit this potential.

The ease with which image processing systems can change existing images challenges ideas about what constitutes an "original" art work. Digital photo illustrations are rapidly destroying our concept of what an original is. Once a collection of picture elements are in the database of an image processing system, they can be manipulated without the loss of image quality known as "generation loss." With a digital image processing system, a copy is no longer inferior to the image it was based upon or copied from. The system also automatically retains a copy when the image is output, and so it is possible to archive[5] these copies. An image can be output again at a later date, and that image will be identical to the one approved the first time, months or even years earlier. What remains in storage is actually less fugitive[6] than a conventional photographic duplicate. . . .

_____

[5]to archive = to put into a collection of records.

[6]fugitive = temporary.

Vocabulary

Look at the reading to help you choose the best answer to each of the following questions.

1. Which phrase in paragraph 1 means "to fill in a missing part"?

2. Which of these words is similar in meaning to *reclaimed* as it is used in paragraph 1?
   a. rescued
   b. regained
   c. restored
   d. realized

3. Which word in paragraph 2 means "a magazine that comes out at regular times"?

4. What is another word for *conventional* in paragraph 3?
   a. standard
   b. exceptional
   c. artistic
   d. natural

5. Which definition of *manipulated* is correct?
   a. controlled for one's own purpose
   b. printed on different kinds of paper
   c. duplicated multiple times
   d. transmitted across long distances

6. In paragraph 4, *anticipated* means _____.
   a. foreseen
   b. desired
   c. needed
   d. demanded

7. The best substitute for the word *emerged* in paragraph 4 is _____.
   a. developed
   b. stopped
   c. appeared
   d. continued

8. Which word in paragraph 5 means "a specific type of art, literature, or music grouped according to a style"?

9. Another way of expressing *potential* as it is used in paragraph 7 would be _____.
   a. matches
   b. possibilities
   c. guarantees
   d. problems

10. Which of these statements is true?
    a. When you *come to grips with* something, you see it for the first time.
    b. *Hold on to* is similar in meaning to *come to grips with.*
    c. *Come to grips with* means to deal with something seriously.
    d. *Run away from* is similar in meaning to *come to grips with.*

Vocabulary Extension

Part A

Match the adjectives with the nouns as they were used in the context of the reading. Look back at the reading to check your answers. Add two more nouns that may be used with each adjective.

    a. boundaries   d. photography
    b. perception   e. process
    c. potential   f. development

1. __d__ digital   *photography*   _____   _____

2. ____ technological   _____   _____   _____

3. ____ preconceived   _____   _____   _____

4. ____ linear   _____   _____   _____

5. ____ human   _____   _____   _____

6. ____ creative   _____   _____   _____

Part B

Use the nouns and adjectives in Part A to complete these sentences about digital art.

1. Photography changes as new _____ _____ are introduced.

2. The computer can open up a lot of _____ _____ for artists.

3. _____ _____ has helped to change the way we view art.

4. Conventional photography is a _____ _____.

5. The mass media have a great influence on _____ _____.

6. We are no longer limited by _____ _____ between art and photography.

Part C

Do you agree or disagree with each of the statements in Part B?

Comprehension

Looking for the Main Ideas

Some of the following statements from the reading are main ideas, and some are supporting statements. Find the statements in the reading. Write M in the blank in front of each main idea. Write S in front of each supporting statement.

_____ 1. The history of photography has always followed the path of technological developments.

_____ 2. Industrial and commercial applications have even influenced the size and shape of photographs.

_____ 3. Digital images have specific advantages over material ones.

_____ 4. Photomontage emerged in the nineteenth century.

_____ 5. Images on a screen form our knowledge of the world today.

_____ 6. All image processing systems are founded on the same idea.

_____ 7. The ease with which image processing systems can change existing images challenges ideas about what constitutes an "original" art work.

_____ 8. With a digital image processing system, a copy is no longer inferior to the image it was based upon or copied from.

Skimming and Scanning for Details

Scan the reading quickly to complete the following sentences. Fill in the blanks.

1. The invention of photography occurred in _____.

2. Paul Delaroche declared, " _____."

3. With digital images, a photograph is as plastic as a _____.

4. With photogravure, books and _____ began to use pictures.

5. Technology became available to everyone with push button cameras and fast _____.

6. Digital images can be easily transmitted, manipulated, and _____.

7. Artists and _____ have been using various techniques for over a hundred years.

8. Photomontage emerged in the _____ _____.

9. Any picture, whether it is a _____, a _____, or a photograph, can be turned into the binary data understood by a computer.

10. Digital photo illustrations are destroying our concept of what is an _____.

Making Inferences and Drawing Conclusions

Some of the following statements are facts from the reading. Other statements can be inferred from the reading. Write F in the blank in front of each factual statement. Write I in front of each inference.

_____ 1. Digital images have changed conventional photography.

_____ 2. Photography has developed with the advance of technology.

_____ 3. Digital images are superior to conventional photographs.

_____ 4. Forms of art never tell the truth.

_____ 5. Digital photo illustration can only work with a computer.

_____ 6. It is possible for all of us to create our own art by using a computer.

_____ 7. Digital photo illustrations should be considered an original form of art.

_____ 8. A copy made from a digital image is not inferior to the image it was based upon.

Discussion

Discuss these questions with your classmates.

1. What do you think of digital photo illustration?
2. Do you think a digital photo illustration should be considered an "original" work of art, or should anyone be able to copy it?
3. How do you think computers and television will change art in the future?

Writing a Summary

Write a one-paragraph summary of Reading 1. Check your summary with the Summary Checklist on page 273.

Paraphrasing

Paraphrase paragraph 2 (The history . . .) of Reading 2. Look at pages 267–270 to find out about paraphrasing. Begin paraphrasing with "According to Gardiner, . . ." or "Based on Gardiner's book, ..."

Organizing: The Essay

An essay consists of several paragraphs that develop one topic. An essay has three parts:

1. *The Introduction.* The introduction is generally one paragraph that introduces the topic and tells the reader what will follow in the subsequent body paragraphs. The introduction contains the thesis statement, which is the central idea of the essay. The thesis statement usually comes at the end of the introduction.

2. *The Body Paragraph.* The number of body paragraphs depends on the number of main points you want to discuss. The body paragraphs support the thesis statement in the introduction.

3. *The Conclusion.* The concluding paragraph ends the essay. It sums up the main points or restates the thesis statement. It also leaves the reader with a final thought or comment on the topic.

The number of paragraphs an essay should have depends on the depth of the writer's examination of the topic. For this level, essays written in class should contain from two to four paragraphs, as well as an introduction and a conclusion.

Essay Form

Introduction	General Statements
	Thesis Statement
Body Paragraphs	Each body paragraph supports the thesis.
	Body Paragraph A develops a single point related to the thesis.
	Body Paragraph B develops a second point related to the thesis.
	Body Paragraph C develops another point related to the thesis.
Conclusion	The conclusion restates the thesis or summarizes the main points and gives a final comment.

The Introduction

The function of an introduction in an essay is to introduce the topic and present the thesis. An introduction should be interesting enough to make the reader want to continue on to find out what you have to say.

There are several strategies that can help make your introduction more interesting to the reader. Here are some suggestions:

Start with a strong opinion. Starting with a strong opinion can catch the reader's attention because the reader may not have thought of this point of view before.

There are no creatures on earth less practical than humans. And nothing shows our frivolity better than fashion. From women's hoop skirts to men's high hats, fashion victims through the ages have endured the ridiculous, the uncomfortable, and the absolutely dangerous in their desire to be fashionable. Even our feet, which are normally planted firmly on the ground, have suffered the pains of keeping up with the latest craze.

Start with a question. Starting with a question is a way of breaking into a subject. You can then use the rest of the essay, including the thesis statement, to answer the question.

Cleanliness is considered a virtue, but just what does it mean to be clean? As most of us have had the unpleasant occasion to discover, one person's definition can be quite different from another's. From Istanbul to Indianapolis, people have their own ways of keeping clean and their own reasons for doing so.

Start with a quotation. Starting with a quotation can make your introduction lively. The quotation should be directly linked to the main idea of the essay. It might be a well-known saying, a remark from a well-known person, or a line from a song or poem.

"Let me have men about me that are fat," says Shakespeare's Julius Caesar to Marcus Antonius. In Julius Caesar's opinion, fat people are more trustworthy than thin ones—that is, those with a "lean and hungry look," who "are dangerous."

Start with an anecdote. Starting with an anecdote or story makes an abstract idea more real to the reader. The anecdote should be related to the thesis.

Imagine walking on the surface of Mars. You follow the channels where water is believed to have once flowed, hike across the flat plains covered with rocks of all sizes, and jump the basin called Hellas, measuring more than 930 miles across. After you explore the polar caps, you climb the huge volcano Olympus Mons, which is twice as high as Earth's highest peak. Seem impossible? It may be in the real world, but not in virtual reality.

An introduction has two parts:

1. General statements

2. Thesis statement

General Statements

The first sentence in an introductory paragraph should be a very general statement about the topic. Its purpose is to get the reader's attention (see the above introductions) and to give background information on the topic. Each statement that follows the general statement should be more specific than the one before it, usually ending with the thesis statement. Your introduction, therefore, will have a funnel shape, as shown in the diagram below.

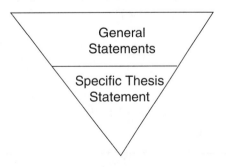

General
Statements

Specific Thesis
Statement

Thesis Statement

The thesis statement is usually the last sentence in the introduction. It is also the most important sentence in the introduction. A thesis statement gives the specific topic and central idea of the whole essay. It states the writer's approach to (method of organization) or attitude toward the central idea and may list the subtopics that will be discussed in the body paragraphs. Each of the topic sentences in the body paragraphs should relate to the thesis statement.

Remember these points about a thesis statement:

1. It states the main topic.

2. It may list subdivisions of the topic.

3. It may indicate the method of organization.

The thesis statement should

*   be expressed in a complete sentence.

*   express an opinion, an idea, or a belief. (It should not be a plain fact.)

Example:

Not a thesis statement: Diet colas contain artificial sweeteners.

Thesis statement: Artificial sweeteners in diet colas may be dangerous to one's health.

*   express only one idea about a topic. (If it expresses more than one idea, the essay will lack unity.)

Example:

Not a thesis statement: Advertising on American television is becoming more sophisticated, and there are some interesting movies.

Thesis statement: Advertising on American television is becoming more sophisticated.

*   not just announce a topic.

Example:

Not a thesis statement: I am going to write about traffic problems in Thailand.

Thesis statement: Traffic problems in Thailand disrupt people's lives.

Read the following sentences. Some are thesis statements, and some are not. Put a check mark next to each thesis statement.

_____ 1. Art has played a vital role in society since the earliest cave dwellers painted scenes on cave walls.

_____ 2. Art today is more varied than at any other time in history, and art is one way to help people with emotional problems.

_____ 3. Art is a form of human expression and thus a means of fulfilling an important human need.

_____ 4. I am going to write about the function of art during the Renaissance.

_____ 5. We can enrich our lives by developing a more active appreciation of the art we live with.

_____ 6. For children, painting and drawing are play activities.

_____ 7. *Folk art* is a term applied to works made by individuals with no academic training in art.

_____ 8. Folk art is a spontaneous, personal, and appealing form of art.

_____ 9. Modern artists enjoy much greater freedom than artists of even a few generations ago, and photography is now considered an art form of its own.

_____10. The social role of artists has changed over time.

_____11. A patron is a person who buys or orders works of art.

_____12. Without patrons, artists could not prosper.

Read the following introductory paragraphs and answer the questions that follow.

1. There is a difference between being an onlooker and being a true observer of art. Onlookers just walk by a work of art, letting their eyes record it while their minds are elsewhere. They have no true appreciation of art. Observers, on the other hand, are informed and appreciative. They have spent the time and energy to educate themselves so that art will be meaningful. They don't just exist side by side with art; they live with it and are aware of its existence in even the smallest part of their daily lives.

   a. What is the topic?

   b. What is the thesis statement?

   c. What device is used to catch the reader's interest?

2. What is art? People in the past always thought they knew what art was. Today, however, art is harder to define. Art in this century is far more complex, for several different reasons. People are exposed to the art of many times and cultures. Much of modern art is difficult to classify. And to further complicate things, we now have works of art created in media undreamed of a few decades ago, including electronic images that may disappear within moments of their creation. It's no wonder that people are asking what exactly art is and isn't and how we can tell the difference.

   a. What is the topic?

   b. What is the thesis statement?

   c. What device is used to catch the reader's interest?

3. "The only difference between me and a madman is that I am not mad," said Salvador Dali, probably the most famous Surrealist artist. Like many other modern artists, such as Vincent van Gogh, Edvard Munch, and Jean Dubuffet, Dali was interested in the relationship between madness and creativity. Certainly the works of these artists, with their swirling lines, strange scenes, and fantastic

dreamlike quality, appear to be the products of unstable minds. Van Gogh produced a whole body of work while in an asylum, so the question of whether madness contributed to his work, and might even have been the force behind it, is a valid one. Where does creativity end and madness begin? Is the line that separates them so thin as to be unrecognizable? These are questions that must be explored in any study of the relationship between madness and creativity in the world of art.

    a.   What is the topic?

    b.   What is the thesis statement?

    c.   What device is used to catch the reader's interest?

The Body Paragraphs

The number of paragraphs in the body of an essay written for this class may range from two to four. The function of the body paragraphs is to explain or prove the thesis statement.

Remember the following points about body paragraphs:

1. *The main idea of the body paragraph should support the thesis statement.* If the thesis statement is about the advantages of exercise—"Regular exercise is beneficial to health"—then the topic sentence of each body paragraph should be about *how* regular exercise is beneficial to health.

2. *Each body paragraph should discuss one aspect of the thesis.* If you are writing about the benefits of exercise, then each body paragraph might discuss one benefit of exercise for health.

3. *The body paragraphs should follow a logical order.* The order of the paragraphs is determined by the type of organization you are using. Each body paragraph should follow the other smoothly through the use of transitions.

Once you have written a thesis statement, you can develop the topics for the body paragraphs in several ways, depending on your thesis statement. You can focus each body paragraph on one of the reasons, steps in a process, advantages and disadvantages, causes, effects, examples, or points of comparison and contrast.

A simple way of developing body paragraphs is to look at the central idea of the thesis statement and turn it into a question. The answers to the question will help you decide on the body paragraphs.

Example:

Thesis statement: Regular exercise is beneficial to health.

Question: In what way is regular exercise beneficial to health?

Answers:
Exercise is good for blood circulation.
It burns up extra calories.
It keeps the body and muscles flexible.

The central idea of the thesis statement is *beneficial to health.* Asking the question "in what way?" provides the answers above. Each body paragraph could focus on a different benefit of exercise.

In the following example, the body paragraphs could deal with points of similarity.

Example:

Thesis statement: Hawaii and Alaska have some similarities.

Question: What similarities?

Answers:
Both are not connected to the forty-eight contiguous states.
Both have a large population of native peoples.
Both are expensive states in which to live.

Exercise 3

Following each thesis statement are two supporting topic sentences that relate to the question that is being asked. Write a third topic sentence.

1. *Thesis:* There are advantages to having a small family.

   Topic sentences:

   I. Parents can afford more things.

   II. Making family decisions is easier.

   III. _____.

2. *Thesis:* Watching television has harmful effects on society.

   Topic sentences:

   I. Family members no longer talk to each other.

   II. People lose interest in their communities.

   III. _____.

3. *Thesis:* New York and Los Angeles differ in many ways.

   Topic sentences:

   I. There are climatic differences.

   II. There are differences in cultural life.

   III. _____ .

4. *Thesis:* Computers have benefited society in several ways.

   Topic sentences:

   I. Operations can be done faster.

   II. Fewer workers are needed, saving money for employees.

   III. _____ .

5. *Thesis:* There are advantages to stopping smoking.

   Topic sentences:

   I. You can have a better social life.

   II. You can get back your self-esteem.

   III. _____ .

The Conclusion

The final paragraph, or conclusion, should make the reader feel that you have completed what you set out to do in your thesis statement. The conclusion is often introduced or signaled by a transition, such as "in conclusion," "to sum up," or "thus."

A conclusion consists of

- a restatement of the thesis in different words

   or

- a restatement of the main points of the essay and a final comment on the subject, based on what you have written.

What you say in the conclusion depends on what ideas you developed in your essay. Do not, however, bring up a new topic in the conclusion.

Read the following introduction and sample concluding paragraph.

There is a difference between being an onlooker and being a true observer of art. Onlookers just walk by a work of art, letting their eyes record it while their minds are elsewhere. They have no true appreciation of art. Observers, on the other hand, are informed and appreciative. They have spent the time and energy to educate themselves so that art will be meaningful. They don't just exist side by side with art; they live with it and are aware of its existence in even the smallest part of their daily lives.

In conclusion, onlookers are unaware and unappreciative of the art surrounding them in their daily lives. Observers, having educated themselves, are able to admire, enjoy, and appreciate art at any level, from a bold and imaginative magazine advertisement to an architecturally classic public building to an Impressionist painting in an art museum. Rather than allow the rich visual world to slip by them, observers pause to let their eyes and minds absorb artistic images of all kinds. Their deep appreciation of artistic expression stretches their intellectual and emotional experiences, thus opening up new areas of enjoyment.

Exercise 4

Read the following introductions and write your own concluding paragraphs.

1. What is art? People in the past always thought they knew what art was. Today, however, art is harder to define. Art in this century is far more complex, for several different reasons. People are exposed to the art of many times and cultures. Much of modern art is difficult to classify. And to further complicate things, we now have works of art created in media undreamed of a few decades ago, including electronic images that may disappear within moments of their creation. It's no wonder that people are asking what exactly art is and isn't and how we can tell the difference.

2. "The only difference between me and a madman is that I am not mad," said Salvador Dali, probably the most famous Surrealist artist. Like many other modern artists, such as Vincent van Gogh, Edvard Munch, and Jean Dubuffet, Dali was interested in the relationship between madness and creativity. Certainly the works of these artists, with their swirling lines, strange scenes, and fantastic dreamlike quality, appear to be the products of unstable minds. Van Gogh produced a whole body of work while in an asylum, so the question of whether madness contributed to his work, and might even have been the force behind it, is a valid one. Where does creativity end and madness begin? Is the line that separates them so thin as to be unrecognizable? These are questions that must be explored in any study of the relationship between madness and creativity in the world of art.

Video Activity • Jackson Pollock, Modern Artist

1. The video describes the life and art of Jackson Pollock (1912–1956), a contemporary of Frida Kahlo who had some similar personality traits. Can you guess what a few of those traits might be?

2. Review the following adjectives used in the video: *daunting, colossal, unbridled, irreverent.*

3. As you watch the video, listen for the information you need to decide whether each statement is true or false.

   a. Just under a hundred of Pollock's paintings were displayed at the Museum of Modern Art in New York.

   ____ T   ____ F

   b. One of Pollock's greatest contributions was to make people think that they too can create art.

   ____ T   ____ F

   c. Before he started a painting, Pollock decided whether it would be hung horizontally or vertically.

   ____ T   ____ F

   d. Pollock's work was acclaimed in the United States but not internationally.

   ____ T   ____ F

   e. Pollock suffered a fatal automobile accident when he was only 44.

   ____ T   ____ F

4. What is your reaction to Pollock's paintings? Do you consider them examples of great art? Why or why not? Write a journal entry or composition in which you summarize the information in the video and then state your own opinions about Pollock's art.

Internet Activity

- Use the Internet to find out about one of these artists: Wassily Kandinsky, Georges Braques, Barbara Hepworth, Louise Bourgeois. What kind of art did the artist create? When and where did he or she live? Tell the class what you found out about the artist's life and art.

- Which web site would you recommend to your class to find out about artists and their art?

CHAPTER TWO

Language

Heere bigynneth the Knyghtes Tale.
Whilom, as olde stories tellen us,
Ther was a duc that highte Theseus;
Of Atthenes he was lord and governour;
And in his tyme swich a conquerour
That gretter was ther noon under the sonne.

Here begins the Knight's Tale.
Once, as old stories tell, there was a prince
Named Theseus that in Athens ruled long since,
A conqueror in his time; for rich lands won
There was no greater underneath the sun.

Pre-Reading Questions

Discuss these questions.

1. Look at the manuscript written in old English and the modern translation. Which words are spelled differently today?

2. There were no spelling rules when old English was spoken. What problems do you think people had as a result of this?

3. Do you think spelling rules are important? Why or why not?

4. What spelling rules do you know in English?

Activity

1. Six words in the list below are spelled wrong. Find the misspelled words and correct them. Use a dictionary to check your answers.

   a. pronunciation (the way you say a word)
   b. batchelor (unmarried male)
   c. superintendant (manager)
   d. exerpt (selected passage from a book or film)
   e. absorption (process of being absorbed)
   f. tarrif (import fee)
   g. occurence (happening)
   h. newstand (place where you buy newspapers and magazines)
   i. separate (to move apart)
   j. nighttime (at night)

2. Do you know the American and British spellings of these words?

American	British
color	
	centre
	behaviour
theater	
jail	
	judgement
program	
	skilful
check	
draft	

Spell It in English

English spelling is confusing and chaotic, as any student of English knows all too well. "How can the letters *ough* spell so many different sounding words," they ask, "like *dough, bough, rough,* and *through*?" And what about a word like *colonel,* which clearly contains no *r* yet pretends it does, and *ache,* with its *k* sound instead of the *chuh* sound of *arch*? And why does *four* have a *u* while *forty* doesn't? There are no simple rules for English spelling, but there is an explanation behind its complexity. We have only to look back in history.

The British Isles

Over the centuries, the English language has been like a magnet, attracting words from numerous other languages. It all started with the Britons, an ancient people living in a part of western Europe that eventually became the British Isles.[1] The Britons spoke a language called Celtic, which was a combination of the early forms of Irish,[2] Scottish,[3] and Welsh.[4] When the Britons were conquered by the Romans and later the Germanic tribes, their language was also invaded. The merging of the languages gave birth to Old English (an early form of the Modern English we know), and a Latin alphabet replaced, with a few exceptions, the ancient Germanic alphabet. In the ninth century, the conquering Norsemen from Scandinavia added their pinch of language spice,[5] as did the French in the 11th century.

---

[1]the British Isles = Great Britain (England, Scotland, Wales) and Ireland.

[2]Irish = the language of Ireland.

[3]Scottish = the language of Scotland.

[4]Welsh = the language of Wales.

[5]pinch of language spice = little bit of variety in the language.

By the 14th century, English, with its mix of at least five languages, had evolved into what is called Middle English and had become Britain's official language. At that time, however, its spellings were far from consistent or rational. Many dialects had developed over the centuries, and sometimes people adopted the spelling used in one part of the country and the pronunciation used in another. For instance, today we use the western English spellings for *busy* and *bury,* but we give the first the London pronunciation *bizzy* and the second the Kentish[6] pronunciation *berry.* Of course, this all happened when English was primarily a spoken language, and only scholars knew how to read and write. Even they appear to have been quite indifferent to matters of consistency in spelling and were known to spell the same word several different ways in a single sentence.

Even after William Caxton set up England's first printing press in the late 15th century and the written word became available to everyone, standard spelling wasn't considered very important. As a matter of fact, the typesetters in the 1500s made things even worse by being very careless about spelling. If a blank space needed to be filled in or a line was too long, they simply changed the spellings of words to make them fit. Moreover, many of the early printers in England were from Germany or Holland and didn't know English very well. If they didn't know the spelling of a word, they made up one! Different printers each had their favorite spellings, so one word might be spelled five or six different ways, depending on who printed the passage.

Throughout this period, names and words appear in many different forms. For instance, *where* can be found as *wher, whair, wair, wheare, were,* and so on. People were even very liberal about their names. More than 80 spellings of Shakespeare's name have been found, among them *Shagsspeare, Shakspeare,* and even *Shakestaffe.* Shakespeare himself didn't spell his name the same way in any two of his six known signatures—he even spelled his name two different ways in his will.

By the late 16th century and early 17th century, some progress had been made in standardizing spelling due to the work of various scholars. By then, however, English spelling was far from a simple phonetic system. For one thing, word pronunciations had changed too rapidly for a truly phonetic spelling to keep up. Also, English had borrowed from many languages and ended up having far too many sounds (more than 40) for the 26 letters in its Roman alphabet. By the time printing houses finally began to agree on standard spellings, many

---

[6]Kentish = of Kent, a county in Southeast England.

of these written forms were only a shadow of their spoken selves. In other words, spelling and pronunciation sometimes had little in common.

Finally, in 1755, Samuel Johnson gave English its first great dictionary. His choice of spellings may not have always been the best or the easiest, but the book helped to make the spellings of most English words uniform. Eventually, people became aware of the need for "correct" spelling. Meanwhile, on the other side of the Atlantic, Noah Webster was standardizing American English in his *American Dictionary of the English Language* and *American Spelling Book.* Although the British had been complaining about the messiness of English spelling for some time, it was the Americans, with their fanaticism for efficiency, who screamed the loudest. Webster not only favored a simplified, more phonetic spelling system, but also tried to persuade Congress to pass a law making the use of nonstandard spelling a punishable offense.

Mark Twain[7] was of the same mind—but laziness figured into his opinion. He wasn't concerned so much with the difficulty of spelling words as with the trouble in writing them. He became a fan of the "phonographic alphabet," created by Isaac Pitman, the inventor of shorthand—a system in which symbols represent words, phrases, and letters. "To write the word 'laugh,'" Twain wrote in *A Simplified Alphabet,* "the pen has to make fourteen strokes—no labor is saved to penman." But to write the same word in the phonographic alphabet, Twain continued, the pen had to make just three strokes. As much as Twain would have loved it, Pitman's phonographic alphabet never caught on.

Interest in reforming English spelling continued to gain momentum on both sides of the Atlantic. For a while, it seemed as if every famous writer and scholar had jumped on the spelling bandwagon.[8] Spelling reform associations began to pop up everywhere. In 1876, the American Philological Association called for the "urgent" adoption of 11 new spellings: *liv, tho, thru, wisht, catalog, definit, gard, giv, hv, infinit,* and *ar.* In the same year, the Spelling Reform Association was formed, followed three years later by a British version.

In 1906, the philanthropist Andrew Carnegie gave $250,000 to help establish the Simplified Spelling Board. The board quickly issued a list of 300 words that were commonly spelled two ways, such as *ax* and *axe,* and called for using the simpler of the two. The board helped to gain

---

[7]Mark Twain = an American author (1835–1910) who wrote many books, including *The Adventures of Tom Sawyer* and *The Adventures of Huckleberry Finn.*

[8]jump on the bandwagon = join a popular movement.

acceptance for quite a few American spellings, including *catalog, demagog,* and *program.*

Eventually the Simplified Spelling Board got carried away with its work, calling for such spellings as *tuff, def, troble,* and *yu.* The call for simplified spelling quickly went out of fashion, particularly with the onset of World War I and the death of Andrew Carnegie. The movement never died out completely, however. Spelling reform continued to be an ongoing, if less dramatic, process, as it had been for centuries. Without the benefit of large donations or outside agencies, many words have shed useless letters. *Deposite* has lost its *e,* as have *fossile* and *secretariate. Musick* and *physick* have dropped their needless *k*'s, and *catalogue* and *dialogue* have shed their last two vowels.

As long as the world goes around, language will continue to change. New words will be added to English; spellings will be altered. But because people are most comfortable with the familiar, it's not likely that we'll ever see a major change in the way most words are spelled. Anyway, what would we do without the challenge of English spelling?

Vocabulary

Select the letter of the answer that is closest in meaning to the italicized word or phrase.

1. The *merging* of the different languages gave birth to Old English.
   a. crossing
   b. confusion
   c. blending
   d. complication

2. By the 14th century, English, with its mix of languages, had *evolved* into what is called Middle English.
   a. improved
   b. appeared
   c. spread
   d. developed

3. Even scholars were quite *indifferent to* matters of consistency in spelling and were known to spell the same word several different ways in a single sentence.
   a. uncaring about
   b. superior about
   c. unsocial about
   d. confused about

4. People were even *liberal* about the spelling of their names, using different spellings on the same page.
   a. receptive
   b. interested
   c. understanding
   d. free

5. Americans, with their *fanaticism* for efficiency, complained the most about the messiness of English spelling.
   a. spirit
   b. obsession
   c. excitement
   d. fascination

6. Interest in reforming English spelling continued to *gain momentum* on both sides of the Atlantic.
   a. be temporary
   b. become stable
   c. grow stronger
   d. get weak

7. The *philanthropist* Andrew Carnegie gave $250,000 to help establish the Simplified Spelling Board.
   a. person who is an expert in language
   b. person who actively helps others
   c. person famous for his or her written work
   d. person known for his or her wealth

8. The Spelling Board outlived its usefulness when it *got carried away with* its work.
   a. became overenthusiastic about
   b. was removed from
   c. got to continue
   d. became successful in

9. The call for simplified spelling went out of fashion with the *onset* of World War I.
   a. outcome
   b. tragedy
   c. end
   d. start

10. Many words *shed* useless letters.
    a. changed
    b. kept
    c. dropped
    d. added

Vocabulary Extension

Part A

Match the adjectives with the nouns as they were used in the context of the reading. Look back at the reading to check your answers. Add two more nouns that may be used with each adjective.

a. change   c. language   e. system
b. offense   d. process   f. spelling

1. _c_ official   <u>language</u>   _____   _____

2. ____ standard   _____   _____   _____

3. ____ punishable   _____   _____   _____

4. ____ phonetic   _____   _____   _____

5. ____ ongoing   _____   _____   _____

6. ____ major   _____   _____   _____

Part B

Use the nouns and adjectives you listed in Part A to complete these sentences about English spelling.

1. Spelling reform continues to be an _____ _____.

2. _____ _____ was introduced with the first dictionaries.

3. It is unlikely that there will be any _____ _____ in English spelling now.

4. Spelling did not represent the _____ _____ of English.

5. Middle English became the _____ _____ of Britain by the 14th century.

6. Webster wanted to make the use of nonstandard spelling a _____ _____.

Part C

Now make new sentences using the adjective and noun combinations you chose in Part A.

Comprehension

Looking for the Main Ideas

Circle the letter of the best answer.

1. What is the main idea of paragraph 3?
   a. By the time English had become a written language, the influence of several languages and dialects had made spelling and pronunciation very inconsistent.
   b. Scholars didn't help the problem of spelling inconsistency because they often spelled words several different ways.
   c. In Britain, English words had different spellings and pronunciations in different parts of the country.
   d. By the 14th century, English had evolved into Middle English and was Britain's official language.

2. Paragraph 6 is mostly about
   a. how progress had been made in standardizing spelling by the 17th century.
   b. why English spelling and pronunciation were often very different.
   c. how English had many more sounds than it had letters in its alphabet.
   d. why printing houses played a role in standardizing spelling.

3. Paragraph 12 is mainly concerned with
   a. the work of the Simplified Spelling Board.
   b. why the call for simplified spelling went out of fashion.
   c. the many words that have been shortened by dropping useless letters.
   d. the ongoing changes in the English language.

Skimming and Scanning for Details

Scan the reading quickly to find the answers to the following questions. Write complete answers.

1. According to the reading, what combination of languages formed the Celtic language?

2. Name four conquering peoples whose languages affected the development of the English language.

3. Before the invention of the printing press, English was mostly what kind of language?

4. Why were the typesetters of the 1500s not very helpful when it came to making spelling standard?

5. Who was responsible for giving English its first great dictionary?

6. What kind of spelling system did Noah Webster favor?

7. What is shorthand and who invented it?

8. What purpose did spelling reform associations serve?

9. In the last sentence of paragraph 11, to what does the last *their* refer?

10. Why are we not likely to see major changes in the way most words are spelled?

Making Inferences and Drawing Conclusions

The answers to these questions are not directly stated in the reading. Circle the letter of the best answer.

1. The reading implies that
   a. conquering tribes forced the Britons to speak their languages.
   b. English was a "pure" language before the 14th century.
   c. the influence of other languages made English a rich but complicated language.
   d. when Britain made English its official language, it stopped foreign words from entering the language and making it even more complicated.

2. From the reading, it can be concluded that
   a. scholars weren't much more educated than the masses.
   b. until the first dictionaries were written, even educated people weren't overly concerned with the spelling of words.
   c. the invention of the printing press didn't have a significant influence on the English language.
   d. there was no real need for an English dictionary before Johnson wrote his in 1755.

3. It can be inferred from the reading that
   a. if it weren't for Mark Twain, many English words would now be spelled differently.
   b. Andrew Carnegie never played a significant role in the area of American spelling.
   c. spelling reform associations had less influence on English spelling changes than the natural course of language changes today.
   d. thanks to many concerned people, spelling is simpler now than it was 200 years ago.

4. The author's tone is
   a. informal.   c. insincere.
   b. sentimental.   d. argumentative.

Discussion

Discuss these questions with your classmates.

1. How would you simplify English spelling?
2. Why do you think proposals to reform English spelling have not won support?
3. If a spelling system based on pronunciation were devised in English, on whose pronunciation would you base it?
4. Do you know any special strategies for remembering difficult spellings in English?
5. Do you know of any new spellings of words used on the Internet?

Coconut and Satellite

The following extracts are taken from the book Great Expressions *by Marvin Vanoni (William Morrow & Co., New York, 1989). They illustrate the historical development of the words* coconut *and* satellite.

Coconut

Portuguese parents of the sixteenth century threatened their children with the bogeyman[1] if they didn't behave. They called the bogeyman *coco*, from a Latin expression meaning "skull."[2] No child had ever actually seen a *coco*, but they knew it had an ugly face.

The Portuguese traders who first arrived at the Pacific Islands found a variety of palm trees that bore a large brown nut about the same size as a man's head. They were shocked to see three black marks on the nut—two eyes and a mouth. It resembled a bogeyman so much that they called it *coconut*. The word was soon adopted by the English and is still with us today.

Satellite

No other city, ancient or modern, can be compared with Rome in terms of world domination. For a period of more than a thousand years the metropolis was the hub of Western civilization. Eventually, however, the very life of the Empire was threatened by economic unrest and a series of rapid changes in government.

---

[1]bogeyman = an imaginary monster used to threaten children.
[2]skull = the bone of the head.

Matters reached such a state that no person of importance dared to walk the streets of the capital without an escort. Many notables were literally surrounded by armed bodyguards; members of such a guard were known as satellites, from an old name for an "attendant."

Despite their satellites, one aristocrat after another was murdered. External difficulties multiplied, the Empire crashed, and classical Latin ceased to be the language of commerce and science. But learned men revived the ancient tongue ten centuries later and used it for most formal speech. Among the resurrected terms was *satellite,* which medieval rulers[3] applied to their personal guards.

Johannes Kepler[4] (1571–1630) thought of the king's satellites when he heard about the strange bodies revolving about Jupiter. Discovered by Galileo,[5] the secondary planets hovered about the planet like guards and courtiers[6] encircling a prince. So in 1611 Kepler named them *satellites;* soon the term was applied to all heavenly bodies[7] that revolve about primary masses.[8]

---

[3]medieval rulers = rulers in the period of history between 1100 and 1500.

[4]Johannes Kepler = a German astronomer (1571–1630) who discovered the shape of the planets' orbits around the sun.

[5]Galileo = an Italian astronomer (1564–1642) who was the first to use a telescope. He made several important discoveries, including that of the orbiting planets of Jupiter.

[6]courtiers = officers or attendants of a king or queen.

[7]heavenly bodies = planets, stars, satellites, and the like.

[8]primary masses = planets.

Vocabulary

Look at the reading titled "Satellite" to answer the following questions.

1. Which word is most similar in meaning to *domination* as it is used in paragraph 1?
   a. government   c. power
   b. balance   d. courage

2. Which word in paragraph 1 means "capital city"?

3. Which of these words is closest in meaning to *hub* as used in the reading?
   a. mystery   c. spectacle
   b. center   d. origin

4. Which word in paragraph 1 means "dissatisfaction"?

5. What is an *escort*, as used in paragraph 2?
   a. a weapon used for protection
   b. a person who guards another
   c. a person who entertains others
   d. a special kind of protection people wore

6. Which of these statements is true?
   a. Notables are famous or important people.
   b. Notables are people who worked for the government.
   c. Notables are royalty.
   d. Notables are educated people.

7. Which of the following is closest in meaning to the phrase *literally surrounded* in paragraph 2?
   a. actually surrounded
   b. surrounded by educated people
   c. surrounded according to writings
   d. almost surrounded

8. What is the meaning of the word *ceased* as used in paragraph 3?
   a. was terminated
   b. completed
   c. stopped
   d. concluded

9. What word in paragraph 3 is similar in meaning to *resurrected*?

10. What does *hovered about* in paragraph 4 mean?
    a. moved around in the air
    b. moved cautiously about
    c. stayed in the air in one place
    d. stayed in a line in the air

Vocabulary Extension

Part A

Read the list of verbs below. Find verbs in the readings that have the same meaning.

1. look like   <u>resemble</u>

2. take up   _____

3. endanger   _____

4. encircle   _____

5. bring back to life   _____

6. move in a circle   _____

Part B

Use the verbs you listed in Part A to complete these questions.

1. Whom do you most _____?

2. What expressions have you recently _____?

3. What fashions have been _____ recently?

4. How many planets that _____ around the sun can you name?

5. What _____ our planet the most?

6. What kinds of people usually _____ movie stars, princes, and presidents?

With a partner, take turns asking and answering these questions.

Comprehension

Looking for the Main Ideas

Some of the following statements from the readings are main ideas, and some are supporting statements. Write M in the blank in front of each main idea. Write S in front of each supporting statement.

_____ 1. Portuguese parents of the 16th century threatened their children with the bogeyman if they didn't behave.

_____ 2. No child had ever actually seen a *coco*, but they knew it had an ugly face.

_____ 3. No other city, ancient or modern, can be compared with Rome in terms of world domination.

_____ 4. For a period of more than a thousand years, the metropolis was the hub of Western civilization.

_____ 5. Johannes Kepler thought of the king's satellites when he heard about the strange bodies revolving about Jupiter.

_____ 6. Discovered by Galileo, the secondary planets hovered about the planet like guards and courtiers encircling a prince.

_____ 7. So in 1611 Kepler named them satellites; soon the term was applied to all heavenly bodies that revolve around primary masses.

Skimming and Scanning for Details

Scan the readings quickly to complete the following sentences.

1. The Portuguese word for bogeyman was _____, a word taken from a Latin expression meaning _____.

2. The Portuguese traders thought the three black marks on the palm nut looked like _____.

3. The Portuguese traders called the palm nut a _____ because they thought it looked like _____.

4. The Roman empire was threatened by _____ and rapid changes in _____.

5. Life became so dangerous for aristocrats that they dared not _____.

6. Important people began to surround themselves with _____, who became known as satellites.

7. The word *satellite* came from an old word for _____.

8. When the Roman empire was destroyed, the Latin language stopped being used for _____ and _____.

9. When the Latin language was revived after centuries, medieval rulers used the word *satellite* to refer to their _____.

10. _____ gave the name *satellite* to the heavenly bodies revolving about _____.

Making Inferences and Drawing Conclusions

Some of the following statements are facts taken from the readings. Other statements can be inferred from the readings. Write F in the blank in front of each factual statement. Write I in front of each inference.

_____ 1. Sixteenth-century Portuguese parents tried to frighten their children into behaving.

_____ 2. Latin has been one of the most influential languages in the world.

_____ 3. Childhood experiences influence our behavior throughout our lives.

_____ 4. The Portuguese traders saw a resemblance between the palm nut and the dreaded *coco* of their childhood.

_____ 5. The Portuguese traders had vivid imaginations.

_____ 6. Many years after Latin was no longer spoken, it influenced English and other languages.

_____ 7. Throughout history, no other city has had the power of Rome.

_____ 8. Even the greatest civilization can fall into ruin.

_____ 9. Rome was destroyed by both internal and external forces.

_____ 10. As time goes on, sometimes words become more generalized in their meaning.

Discussion

Discuss these questions with your classmates.

1. Certain English words are formed by combining parts of two other words, usually the first part of one and the last part of another. An example is *smog,* which is a combination of *smoke* and *fog.* Other examples include *brunch* and *motel.* Words formed with this technique are called *portmanteau* words. Create five new portmanteau words.

2. Describe the process you would use in learning a new language.

3. Imagine that four of you are together in a deserted part of the world. None of you speaks the same language. Describe the process of creating a language to communicate with one another.

Writing a Summary

Write a one-paragraph summary of Reading 1. Check your summary with the Summary Checklist on page 273.

Paraphrasing

Paraphrase paragraph 1 of "Satellite" in Reading 2. Look at pages 267–270 to find out about paraphrasing. Begin paraphrasing with "According to Vanoni, . . ." or "Based on Vanoni's work, ..."

Research

Choose a process, procedure, or event leading to a change over a period of time. Consult appropriate sources in the library and/or use your own experience or that of friends to gather information.

The following are suggested topics:

How the education system works (in the United States or your country)
How the digestive system works
How a holiday is celebrated (in the United States or your country)
How babies learn to talk
How to learn to use a computer
How you get a divorce
How a volcano explodes

You may use your research later to write a process essay.

Read the following essay written by a student.

The Chinese Art of Writing

Chinese is one of the most remarkable pieces of art in language that humankind has ever made. In elementary school, Chinese teachers ask their students to write not only correctly but beautifully by printing a picture for each character. Chinese is different from western languages such as German, French, or English because it has no alphabet. Instead it contains 50,000 characters. If a person knows 5,000 of the most commonly used characters, he or she can read a newspaper. How many characters a person knows indicates how intellectual that person is. Chinese is one of the world's oldest languages, and its written form, like that of most languages, developed from the pictograph.

Thi Chi is credited with the invention of the written Chinese language 5,000 years ago. He created the first Chinese characters by imitating the shapes of living things in the world. The sign for sun was a circle with a wavy line through it to show heat (⊖). The sign for mountain had three peaks (Ⅲ). The sign for a child was a child reaching for mother (♀). The sign for man looked like a man (⸮). These signs or pictographs could be easily understood because they looked like real things.

Then, after a few centuries, the Chinese made these pictographs easier to draw. The signs were called characters and are used to this day. These are some of the examples of the changes: the character for sun became 日; the character for mountain became 山; and the character for child became 子. Two lines at 120 degrees (人) now represent man.

Later, it became necessary to express more ideas, so strokes were added to the characters or characters were combined. With extra strokes a character had a new meaning. For example, a man with arms outstretched at 180 degrees (大) represents big, and two short lines on each side of a man (小) means small. Characters were combined to make new words, as in the example of the character to bark (口犬), which is made up of the combination of mouth (口) and dog (犬). Another example of this kind is the character for good (好), which is made up of a woman and child because in China, as well as everywhere, a mother with her child is a good thing. Sometimes a character is repeated to make a different word, as in the character for forest (林), which is the repetition of tree (木).

From the first character that Thi Chi created, Chinese words have expanded to more than 10,000. The Chinese language also had an influence on other Asian languages such as Japanese and Korean, which somehow contain some Chinese characteristics. Chinese is not only a tool for people to communicate with but also an important subject for Chinese artists to study. Chinese fine handwriting, or calligraphy, was considered a branch of painting, and calligraphy was often combined with painting in a work of art. Chinese can be considered as one of the most beautiful languages in the world without question.

Chun Che
Taiwan

Student Essay Follow-Up

1. What is the writer trying to do in this essay?
2. Underline the thesis statement.
3. Are time signals used through each phase of the process?
4. Underline the topic sentence in each of the body paragraphs. Are the topic sentences supported?
5. Is the process of development clear?

Organizing: The Process Essay

In Reading 1, we saw how English spelling developed over time into what it is today. In Reading 2, we saw how the words *coconut* and *satellite* originated and how they came to mean what they mean today. Both of these readings use a chronological (time) order.

One type of process essay describes events in the order in which they occurred over a period of time, such as a morning, a day, a childhood, or the duration of a war. A history or a biography usually describes events over a period of time.

Another type of process essay describes a technical process, such as how a computer works or how hair is transplanted or how chocolate is made. (This type of essay contains many verbs in the passive form.)

Yet another type of process essay is the "how to" essay, in which you tell someone how to do or make something. This type is used to discuss topics such as how to prepare a special dish or how to get a driver's license.

The essential component in all process essays is time order. Use time experiences and transition signals to indicate the time sequences clearly.

Thesis Statement for the Process Essay

The thesis statement for a process that is historical should name the process and indicate chronological order through words like *developed* or *evolved.*

Chinese is one of the world's oldest languages, and its written form, like that of most languages, *developed* from the pictograph.

The thesis statement for a technical process should name the process and indicate that it involves a series of steps.

Hair transplantation is a fairly simple process.

It may also name the main steps in the process:

The main steps in the process of hair transplantation are removal of the desired number of hair transplants, removal of small plugs in the bald area, and the insertion of the hair transplants.

The thesis statement for a "how to" essay is the same as the one for a technical process. It should name the process or item and indicate that it involves a number of steps.

Baking your own bread can be quite easy if you follow these steps.

Rescue breathing for a person who is unconscious involves a sequence of steps that must be followed carefully.

Organizing the Process Essay

Deciding how to divide a process essay into paragraphs can be tricky. If you are writing a historical or narrative piece about a chronological process, divide your paragraphs by major time periods, as in the student essay. However, if you are writing about how to do something, the following guidelines will help you:

- *Introduction.* Introduce the topic and explain why the process is performed, by whom it is performed, and in what situation it is performed. You may list the main steps of the process in the order in which they are performed.

- *Body Paragraphs.* Start to describe the process, introducing the first step in a topic sentence. You may at this point state the equipment and supplies needed for the process. Divide the process into three or four major steps. Each major step should be described in a body paragraph. For example, if you were describing a wedding ceremony in your country, the first major step would be the preparations, the next would be the ceremony, and the last would be the reception or banquet.

- *Conclusion.* Summarize by restating the main steps and describing the result. The type of conclusion will depend on the type of process you are describing (see the student essay).

Time Expressions

Time may be indicated by a preposition with a date or historical period: *in 1920, by the 16th century, over the next ten years,* or other time expressions. We will look at some prepositions commonly used with time.

During indicates the duration of the activity from beginning to end, usually without stating the length of time.

> *During* her first year at college, she performed remarkably.

For indicates the length of time or an appointed time.

> I waited *for* an hour.
> My appointment was *for* three o'clock.

Since indicates a period of time from its beginning to the present.

> He has been living there *since* 1920 (He is still there.)

Other prepositions of time indicate when or how long: *as, in, on, to, till, up to, upon, as early as, as soon as, from/to, as late as.*

> The process should be completed *in* three hours.
> The class will have a test *on* Friday.
> He worked *till* ten o'clock.
> She spends *up to* three hours every day rehearsing.
> Leave to thaw for an hour *upon* taking it out of the freezer.
> She woke up *as soon as* it was daylight.
> Cook the beans *from* twenty-five *to* thirty-five minutes.

Dependent clauses can be introduced by prepositions used as adverbs *(after, before, until)* or by adverbs *(when, while):*

> *After* (or *when*) you have made a rough draft, start revising your work.

Before starting on the second draft, make sure that your details support your topic sentences.

Don't forget to look up the spelling of words you are unsure of *when* you are editing.

Do not be distracted *while* you are editing each sentence.

Other useful words that indicate a sequence in a process are ordinal numbers *(first, second, third)* and interrupters *(next, then, later, simultaneously, eventually).* The expressions *previous to, prior to,* and *just before* place an action before another action.

Prior to writing your research, make sure you have all the information at hand.

Next, revise your draft.

Look back at Reading 1 and underline all the words that indicate time or sequence.

Exercise 1

Fill in the blanks using the following time words. Each choice can be used only once.

while	still	for
1561	when	in 1637
until	during	after
in 1499	later	then
in 1542		

The first European to discover the Amazon River was Spanish

explorer Vicente Pinzon _____. He had been on Columbus's

first voyage seven years earlier and was _____ determined to

find a route to the Orient. _____ he sailed into the mouth of

the Amazon and looked at the mighty river ahead of him, he

thought he had gone around the world and hit the Ganges River in

India. He stopped at some islands in the mouth of the river and

_____ sailed on.

Forty-three years _____, _____, Francisco de Orellana became the first European to travel the entire river, although that was not what he set out to do at all. _____ a Spanish expedition became stranded in the jungles of Eastern Peru, Orellana was sent down the Napo River to find food. But starvation, sickness, and Indian attacks took place, and Orellana couldn't get back upriver. Instead, he followed tributaries to the Amazon, and _____ 16 months of incredible hardships, he and what was left of his party made it all the way to the sea.

In _____, the notorious Lope de Aguirre traveled the Amazon _____ on the run from Spanish troops. He left a trail of death and destruction throughout the Amazon all the way to the sea.

No one traveled the entire river _____ another 76 years, _____ a Portuguese captain, Pedro Texeira, became the first to complete an upriver "ascent" _____.

Writing Practice

Choose one of the following topics.

1. Write a process essay, using chronological order or steps, about one of the topics you researched in this chapter.
2. Write a process essay on how you recovered from an illness or accident.
3. Write a process essay on learning a foreign language.
4. Write a process essay on a ceremony in your country (for example, a wedding). Indicate the sequence of steps clearly.

1. Pre-writing.
   Work alone, with a partner, or in a group.
   a. Brainstorm the topic. Look at page 258 to find out about brainstorming. Choose the pre-writing technique you prefer.
   b. Brainstorm how to divide your process essay into three or four parts.
   c. Work on a thesis statement.

2. Develop an outline.
   a. Organize your ideas.
   Step 1: Write your thesis statement.
   Step 2: Divide your steps into three or four paragraphs.
   Step 3: Provide details of each step in the paragraphs.
   b. Make a more detailed outline. The essay outline on page 22 will help you.

3. Write a rough draft.
   Look at page 261 to find out about writing a rough draft.

4. Revise your rough draft.
   Use the checklist on page 262.

5. Edit your essay.
   Check your work for errors in subject and verb agreement. For example, the words *everybody* and *nobody* take a singular verb.

   Example:
   Error: Everybody find English spelling difficult to understand.
   Correct: Everybody finds English spelling difficult to understand.

   When you find a mistake of this type, you can use the symbol "pro agree" (pronoun agreement). Look at page 263 for other symbols to use when editing your work.

6. Write your final copy.

Video Activity • Egyptian Hieroglyphs

1. The video is about the writing system used by the ancient Egyptians—called hieroglyphics—in which pictures—called hieroglyphs—are used to represent sounds or ideas. How is this system similar to or different from the writing system used in your language?

2. Before watching the video, review these words: *tomb* (noun), *decipher* (verb), *posthumous* (adjective), *Coptic* (adjective), *pharaoh* (noun).

3. While watching, make notes that will help you answer the following questions.

   a. Why is it that we can understand the ancient Egyptian writing system but we do not know how it was pronounced?

   b. Where have many examples of ancient Egyptian hieroglyphs been found?

   c. What happened in 1822 that helped us to understand ancient Egyptian hieroglyphs?

   d. Describe the appearance of the hieroglyphs shown in the video.

4. Can you think of advantages and disadvantages of a writing system in which symbols represent meaning, compared to a system in which symbols represent sounds? What other world cultures used hieroglyphics?

Internet Activity

- Find out about the movement for "spelling reform" in English. Who started it? Does it still exist?
- Find a good English or bilingual dictionary on the Internet that you can recommend to your class.

CHAPTER THREE

Hygiene

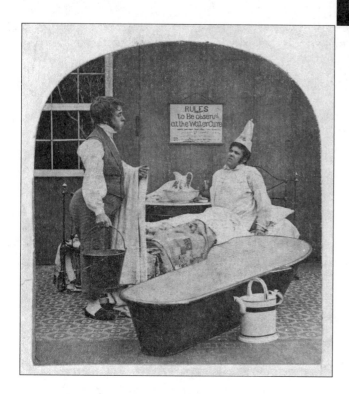

Pre-Reading Questions

Discuss these questions.

1. Look at the picture. Describe how people took a bath in the old days.

2. What reasons are there for taking a bath, in addition to getting clean?

3. What is your opinion of public baths? Why do you think they are important in some cultures?

Activity

Take the following quiz, circling T for true and F for false. Then compare your answers with those of your classmates. When you have finished, check your answers on page 275.

1. The ancient Romans did not place much emphasis on personal cleanliness.   T   F

2. Up until the 1870s in Europe and America, doctors washed their hands only after surgery—not before.   T   F

3. Shrimps clean other fish in the sea.   T   F

4. In colonial Pennsylvania and Virginia, there were laws that forced people to bathe at least once a month.   T   F

5. During the Middle Ages in Europe, people bathed when they were baptized and seldom after that.   T   F

6. For thousands of years, people have been aware that germs cause disease.   T   F

Cleanliness

Cleanliness is considered a virtue, but just what does it mean to be clean? As most of us have had the unpleasant occasion to discover, one person's definition can be quite different from another's. From Istanbul to Indianapolis, people have their own ways of keeping clean and their own reasons for doing so.

Cleanliness has had a long and varied history with mixed reviews. Sometimes it's popular; sometimes it's not. Throughout the ages, personal cleanliness has been greatly influenced by religion, culture, and technology. Moreover, bathing has served many functions in addition to hygiene. Baths are also places for social gathering, mental and physical relaxation, and medicinal treatment. Archaeological evidence suggests that bathing is as old as the first civilizations. Soaplike material has been found in clay jars of Babylonian origin, dating back to about 2800 B.C.E.[1] One of the first known bathtubs came from Minoan Crete, and a pretty sophisticated plumbing system of clay pipes is known to have existed in the great palace of King Minos, built in 1700 B.C.E. The ancient Egyptians didn't have such plumbing expertise but are known to have had a positive attitude toward hygiene. They washed with soapy material made of animal and vegetable oils and salts and sat in a shallow kind of bath while attendants poured water over them.

The Greeks prized cleanliness, although they didn't use soap. Instead, they rubbed oil and ashes on their bodies, scrubbed with blocks of rocks or sand, and scraped themselves clean with a curved metal instrument. A dip in the water and anointment with olive oil followed. They were no doubt clean, but how would they smell if we followed them down the street today?

There were public Grecian baths as well as private ones, but they didn't serve the social purpose of the Roman baths. It seems that no one in history has indulged in bathing the way the Romans did. Nearly

---

[1]B.C.E. = Before Christian Era.

a dozen large and magnificent public bathhouses dotted the city, and many hundreds of private baths were found in homes. Emperor Caracalla's bath could accommodate 1,600 bathers at a time. Emperor Diocletian entertained crowds of more than 3,000 in the marble splendor of his bath, finished in 305 C.E.[2] Apparently the Romans had lots of time on their hands, because bathing was not just an exercise; it was an event. First, a bather entered a warm room to sweat and to engage in lengthy conversations. Fine oils and sand were used to cleanse the body. Next came a hot room where the bather would be treated to even more sweating, splashing with water, more oils and scraping, and yet more talk. Finally, the Romans concluded the process by plunging into a cool and refreshing pool. In the early years of the baths, men and women had separate areas, but eventually the sexes mixed and the baths lost their virtuous purpose.

So corrupt were Roman society and its baths that the fathers of the early Christian church discouraged bathing. The hygienic practices of the Greeks and Romans were repressed to such an extent that Europe during the Middle Ages has been said to have gone a thousand years without a bath. Queen Isabella of Castille boasted that she had bathed only twice in her life—at birth and before her marriage. Religion wasn't the only reason why Europeans didn't bathe. Although the royal and wealthy sometimes indulged, commoners found bathing virtually[3] impossible. With no running water, polluted rivers, and soap taxed as a luxury item, the ordinary citizen had little opportunity to bathe. As a result, people lived in filth,[4] clothing was infested with vermin,[5] and disease was rampant.

Early Americans, being of European origin, brought their dirty habits with them. By the 1800s, however, both Europeans and Americans were reforming their ways. As it became known that filth led to disease, governments began to improve sanitation standards. Wash houses were built, and bathing became a good thing again. In the United States, tubs, water heaters, and good indoor plumbing put bathing within the reach of ordinary citizens. They like it so much that today the average American claims to shower or bathe more than seven times a week.

---

[2]C.E. = Christian Era.

[3]virtually = almost.

[4]filth = very dirty conditions.

[5]vermin = insects that live on the body of humans or animals.

In America, clean means not only free of dirt but free of odor as well—or, rather, human odors, because millions of dollars are spent each year on powders and perfumes that cover up any natural smells that might slip by. As any deodorant ad will tell you, to have body odor (B.O.) is a grave social offense.

In many Middle Eastern countries, cleanliness has religious overtones that link spiritual and physical purification. The Jewish people have many religious laws relating to hygiene, both personal and in the preparation of food. Muslims, too, live by some very strict rules related to cleanliness. For example, they are required to wash certain parts of their bodies, such as their feet and hands, before they pray. Since the time of Mohammed, sweat baths, or *hammams,* have been recommended. They serve not only as places for cleansing but also as retreats and opportunities for socializing. As a matter of fact, the Crusaders,[6] who enjoyed hammams, brought the idea of the public bath back to Europe with them and introduced the use of thermal baths as therapy for a variety of ills.

For many Middle Easterners, baths are a sort of ritual, a major affair that takes longer than an hour. Bathing begins with a steam, followed by rubbing the body with a hard towel, then soaping and rinsing. People usually want to lie down after a bath. Since it takes so long and is so exhausting, they indulge in these baths once a week.

Asian cultures are very strict and ritualistic about their cleanliness. The Japanese in particular are known for their personal hygiene, which extends from removing their shoes and putting on special slippers before entering any house or building to extensive washing before meals.

It is logical to conclude that cleanliness has many different meanings and is judged by a variety of standards. *Clean* mans pure, in a religious sense, as well as clean of body. For some it means being "squeaky clean"[7] and smelling like roses. For others, a more "natural" state is acceptable. Whether it means washing one's hands and face or a head-to-toe scrubbing, cleanliness is a cultural practice, with enough stories and emotions behind it to make a real soap opera.

---

[6]the Crusaders = men who went on military expeditions undertaken by Christian powers in the 11th, 12th, and 13th centuries to win the Holy Land from the Muslims.

[7]squeaky clean = extremely clean.

Vocabulary

Select the letter of the answer that is closest in meaning to the italicized word or phrase.

1. A dip in the water and *anointment with* olive oil followed.
   a. a rub with
   c. a soak in
   b. application of
   d. a wash with

2. No one in history *indulged in* bathing the way the Romans did.
   a. pleased themselves by
   b. made rules against
   c. talked and wrote about
   d. had the patience for

3. The baths lost their *virtuous* purpose.
   a. practical
   c. small
   b. natural
   d. good

4. The hygienic practices of the Greeks and Romans were *repressed*.
   a. encouraged
   c. held back
   b. defined
   d. debated

5. Queen Isabella *boasted* that she had bathed only twice in her life.
   a. said proudly
   c. expressed quickly
   b. argued often
   d. denied strongly

6. The clothing of commoners was often *infested with* vermin.
   a. free of
   c. made by
   b. decorated with
   d. full of

7. Disease was *rampant*.
   a. not commonly found
   c. avoided at all cost
   b. easily controlled
   d. spread everywhere

8. In America, body odor is a *grave* social offense.
   a. serious
   b. harmful
   c. rare
   d. frequent

9. In many Middle Eastern countries, cleanliness has religious *overtones.*
   a. rituals
   b. meanings
   c. controls
   d. results

10. Sweat baths also served as *retreats.*
    a. locations for parties
    b. opportunities to get work accomplished
    c. places to get away and rest
    d. areas in which to exercise

Vocabulary Extension

Part A

Match the adjectives with the nouns as they were used in the context of the reading. Look back at the reading to check your answers. Add two more nouns that may be used with each adjective.

a. treatment   c. overtones   e. relaxation
b. offense   d. hygiene   f. evidence

1. _e_ mental   relaxation   _____   _____

2. ___ medicinal   _____   _____   _____

3. ___ archaeological   _____   _____   _____

4. ___ social   _____   _____   _____

5. ___ religious   _____   _____   _____

6. ___ personal   _____   _____   _____

Part B

Use the nouns and adjectives you listed from Part A to complete these sentences about cleanliness.

1. Ruins of many ancient civilizations show _____ _____ of baths.

2. Bathing is a form of _____ _____.

3. If you are sick, bathing can be a form of _____ _____.

4. In some cultures, bathing is not only for cleanliness; it also has _____ _____.

5. If your body smells, it can be a _____ _____.

6. _____ _____ is more important in some cultures than in others.

Part C

Do you agree with the sentences in Part B? Are they true or false? Give some examples.

Comprehension

Looking for the Main Ideas

Circle the letter of the best answer.

1. What is the main idea of paragraph 2?
    a. Bathing has many different functions in society besides that of cleansing the body.
    b. Indoor plumbing was achieved by the Minoans in Crete almost 4,000 years ago, although their technology didn't immediately spread to other parts of the world.
    c. The Egyptians made up for their lack of sophisticated plumbing by having servants pour water over them while they bathed.
    d. Cleansing of the body has been done for thousands of years in many different ways and for many different reasons.

2. Paragraph 4 is mostly about
    a. the size of the Roman public bathhouses and the emperors who built them.
    b. the social purposes of the Roman baths and their eventually corrupting influence.
    c. the extent, purpose, and rituals of the Roman baths.
    d. the differences between Roman baths and Greek baths.

3. Paragraph 8 is mainly concerned with
    a. Crusaders bringing the idea of public baths to Europe.
    b. religious laws connected with cleanliness in the Middle East.
    c. the importance of sweat baths in some countries.
    d. the use of baths as a treatment for illness.

Skimming and Scanning for Details

Scan the reading quickly to find the answers to these questions. Write complete answers.

1. According to the reading, what three things have influenced the bathing habits of people over the centuries?

2. According to the reading, how were the Greeks different from the Egyptians in their bathing habits?

3. In the last sentence of paragraph 3, what does the word *them* refer to?

4. What bathing rituals were part of the three stages of bathing in the Roman baths?

5. Why did the leaders of the early Christian church discourage bathing?

6. What three problems prevented commoners in Europe from taking baths?

7. What finally prompted Europeans and Americans to change their cleanliness habits?

8. What Muslim tradition influenced the introduction of therapeutic thermal baths in Europe?

9. To what does the word *people* in paragraph 9, sentence 3, refer?

10. What are two hygienic habits of the Japanese?

Making Inferences and Drawing Conclusions

The answers to these questions are not directly stated in the reading. Circle the letter of the best answer.

1. The reading implies that
   a. only the most advanced societies recognized the importance of cleanliness.
   b. cleanliness can mean only one thing: a body free from dirt and odors.
   c. soap and bathtubs have not always been necessary for cleanliness.
   d. little evidence exists regarding the cleanliness habits of early civilizations.

2. From the reading, it can be concluded that
   a. religion has always had a detrimental effect on society's personal cleanliness.
   b. over the ages, some societies have valued personal cleanliness more than others.
   c. during the Middle Ages, Europeans had no need to be concerned with personal cleanliness.
   d. technology has had little effect on Americans' bathing habits.

3. It can be inferred from the reading that
   a. Middle Eastern traditions have had no influence on Western habits of cleanliness.
   b. overwashing can be hazardous to a person's health.
   c. the Grecian baths served a social purpose.
   d. bathing is a ritualistic and meaningful activity that can be viewed in a cultural context.

4. The author's purpose is to
   a. amuse.   c. convince.
   b. inform.   d. dispute.

Discussion

Discuss these questions with your classmates.

1. What is the most usual way of washing or taking a bath in your country?
2. How important are grooming activities such as brushing your teeth or combing your hair?
3. How is body odor regarded in your country and in other countries?
4. What is your definition of cleanliness?

Cleaner Fish

The following passage is from the book Symbiosis *by Nicolette Perry (Blandford Press, Dorsett, Poole, England, 1983). It describes the cleaning habits of fish.*

Figure 1. There are at least 45 species of fish that are known cleaners (engage in cleaning symbiosis with other fish). One example is the goby, which cleans the Nassau Grouper. The Black Surgeon fish goes from black to blue while being cleaned by the *Labroides dimidiatus.*

Cleaning symbioses[1] are found in the sea, in freshwater, on land and in the air, but the greatest number of examples concern marine species. It is essential for all creatures to have some method of keeping themselves clean and free from parasites. If they do not, they will probably fall ill from infected wounds or the effects of disease and blood loss from parasites. For those species that are unable to clean themselves it is obviously vital to find some other animal to perform this cleaning function. This chapter is concerned with describing some typical examples of cleaning symbioses as well as the more extraordinary ones.

The vast majority of cleaners are fish; at least 45 species are known cleaners and there may well be more. Fish that are habitually cleaned often have to modify their usual behavior to allow the cleaners to do their work. It is not normal for aggressive species like shark, barracuda and moray eels to allow small fish to swim safely near them. With known cleaner species, however, these and other fish change their attitude completely and allow the cleaners all over their bodies without displaying any ferocity[2] towards them. The clients will slow down or stop completely (unusual behavior for most fish, as they usually move all the time), open and close their mouths and gill[3] covers and assume awkward-looking postures to help the cleaners. It is

---

[1]symbiosis = the living or working together of two different organisms in a mutually beneficial relationship.

[2]ferocity = fierceness, violence.

[3]gill = the organ through which a fish breathes.

quite possible that some species have become extinct because of an inability to establish a cleaning symbiosis. So many individuals could have fallen foul of ectoparasites,[4] fungi and bacteria that the population was made inviable.

Some fishes change color while being cleaned. Black Surgeon Fish go from black to blue when they are being cleaned by *Labroides dimidiatus.* The Goatfish changes from pale brown to pink while the same cleaner picks it over for parasites.

Fishes being groomed guard their cleaners against danger by warning them of the approach of predators. The Nassau Grouper when cleaned by gobies[5] warns its cleaner by suddenly closing its mouth, leaving only a small gap to allow the goby to escape. Even if the grouper is in imminent danger itself it takes time to warn the goby. This shows the regard that the client feels for its cleaner and the service that it performs.

Several species of cleaner set up cleaning stations in one particular place. The local fish soon realize where the cleaner is located and will visit it whenever they require cleaning. Quite astonishing numbers of fish are cleaned in this way: not only territorial species that would normally be found in the area but also migratory ones which have gone out of their way to visit these stations. Client fish will patiently wait their turn to be cleaned, and even form orderly queues.

Quite a considerable amount of observational and experimental work has been done on these cleaning stations. Limbaugh, for example, discovered that over three hundred fish can be cleaned by a single Senorita Fish in a six-hour period. These fish go back to the same cleaner every few days for another session and this enables them to remain in peak condition.

Limbaugh also did some experiments in waters off the Bahamas. He removed all the cleaner fish from one locality and observed the effects on the species normally found there. Within two days the numbers of fish were severely reduced and within two weeks almost all the territorial fish had disappeared. Those that remained had developed the fuzzy marks that are an indication of fungal infection. It had been shown in previous experiments that the introduction of

---

[4]ectoparasites = parasites that live on the exterior of the host.
[5]gobies = a kind of cleaner fish.

cleaners into an aquarium infected by fungi can restore its inhabitants to health.

From the above the value of cleaning symbiosis in the marine habitat can easily be seen. Without the work of all the cleaners of the ocean, the effects of parasites, fungi and injury would kill many more species than they do already. The Senorita Fish is an example of a typical cleaner. It is of the wrasse family and lives off the coast of California. It is an active, small, cigar-shaped fish that the local people call the Senorita because of its cleaning habits. Its client fishes include the Topsmelt, Black Sea Bass, Opaleye, Blacksmith Fish and many more. These fish are almost all much larger than the cleaner and would normally prey on wrasses of the Senorita's size. They do not attack the Senorita, however, but wait patiently until it is their turn to be cleaned, hold themselves still and often in the most peculiar postures while being attended to. The fish in the area of the coast that the Senorita Fish inhabits are especially troubled by fungal infection, and removal of the white growths caused by the fungi is the cleaner's most important function. The cleaning phenomenon has been observed for many years to the extent that one species is popularly called the Cleaner Fish or Wrasse. It is a small, slim fish with cyan-colored[6] body, striped with darker blue or black. The cleaner fish goes onstage further than the Senorita in that it actively attracts clients by "dancing." It swims in a vertical position, head downwards, and undulates its body from side to side. This is a most unusual posture for fish, as they usually swim horizontally to the sea bed. This "dancing" makes the cleaner noticeable to even the most myopic fish, and it has become the cleaner's trade mark.

Clients line up, as for the Senorita, until it is their turn to be cleaned, and also allow the little fish to enter their mouths and gill cavities unharmed. The contents of various species' stomachs have been examined to assess the quantity of cleaner fish that are eaten, both by fish that are known clients and others. It has been found that very few cleaners are consumed by any species, although fish of similar size make up the bulk of the diet. So few cleaner fish are eaten that it seems probable that the small number that are are taken accidentally by absent-minded clients rather than actively predated upon.

---

[6]cyan-colored = greenish-blue.

Vocabulary

Look at the reading to answer the questions.

1. Which of the following phrases could be substituted for *fallen foul of* in paragraph 2?
   a. been the cause of
   b. been eliminated by
   c. eaten enough of
   d. been harmed by

2. Which of the following is closest in meaning to the word *inviable* as used in paragraph 2?
   a. unable to communicate
   b. unable to survive
   c. unable to move
   d. unable to be eaten

3. Which word in paragraph 4 means "attended to or cared for"?

4. In paragraph 4, what does *imminent* mean?
   a. immediate
   b. constant
   c. great
   d. frequent

5. Which of these words is closest in meaning to *peak* as it is used in paragraph 6?
   a. top
   b. average
   c. inferior
   d. artificial

6. Something fuzzy
   a. is hard and clear.
   b. is covered with fluffy particles.
   c. changes shape.
   d. changes color.

7. In paragraph 8, what does *undulates* mean?
   a. looks right to left as it passes
   b. advances in stops and starts
   c. moves back and forth in a wavy form
   d. swims quickly in a straight line

8. What is the meaning of *myopic* in paragraph 8?

   a. unable to see faraway objects clearly

   b. having sharp eyes and good hearing

   c. able to see in the dark

   d. unable to distinguish large objects

9. Which of these words is closest in meaning to *assess* as used in paragraph 9?

   a. judge   c. confirm

   b. compare   d. view

10. Which phrase in paragraph 9 means "the greater part of"?

Vocabulary Extension

Part A

Match the verbs with the nouns as they were used in the context of the reading. Look back at the reading to check your answers. Add two more nouns that may be used with each verb.

   a. a station   c. ferocity   e. effects
   b. smaller fish   d. behavior   f. a service

1. _d_ modify   behavior   _____   _____

2. ___ display   _____ _____   _____

3. ___ perform   _____ _____   _____

4. ___ set up   _____ _____   _____

5. ___ observe   _____ _____   _____

6. ___ prey on   _____ _____   _____

Part B

Make questions about cleaner fish, using each of the word combinations in Part A.

Example:

How do larger fish *modify* their *behavior?*

With a partner, take turns asking and answering your questions.

Comprehension

Looking for the Main Ideas

Some of the following statements from the reading are main ideas, and some are supporting statements. Write M in the blank in front of each main idea. Write S in front of each supporting statement.

_____ 1. If they do not, they will probably fall ill from infected wounds or the effects of disease and blood loss from parasites.

_____ 2. Fish that are habitually cleaned often have to modify their usual behavior to allow the cleaners to do their work.

_____ 3. With known cleaner species, however, these and other fish change their attitude completely and allow the cleaners all over their bodies without displaying any ferocity towards them.

_____ 4. The clients will slow down or stop completely (unusual behavior for most fish, as they usually move all the time), open and close their mouths and gill covers and assume awkward-looking postures to help the cleaners.

_____ 5. Some fishes change color while being cleaned.

_____ 6. Fishes being groomed guard their cleaners against danger by warning them of the approach of predators.

_____ 7. Even if the grouper is in imminent danger itself it takes time to warn the goby.

_____ 8. Several species of cleaner set up cleaning stations in one particular place.

_____ 9. These fish go back to the same cleaner every few days for another session and this enables them to remain in peak condition.

_____ 10. Within two days the numbers of fish were severely reduced and within two weeks almost all the territorial fish had disappeared.

Skimming and Scanning for Details

Scan the reading quickly to complete the following sentences.

1. Even normally aggressive species like _____, _____, and _____ allow small cleaner fish to swim near them.

2. Some species may have become extinct because of an inability to _____.

3. The Goatfish will change from _____ to _____ while being cleaned by a cleaner fish.

4. The Nassau Grouper warns its cleaner fish that predators are in the area by _____.

5. Many larger fish will not wait for the cleaner fish to come to them. Instead, they _____.

6. In a _____-hour period, a single _____ fish can clean over 300 fish.

7. If cleaner fish are taken out of an area they usually inhabit, the client fish that remain after the others have left the area will _____.

8. If cleaner fish are put in an aquarium with fish infected by _____, the cleaner fish can _____.

9. The cleaner fish, or Wrasse, attracts clients by doing a dance that involves _____.

10. In appearance, the Senorita Fish is _____ and _____ -shaped.

Making Inferences and Drawing Conclusions

Some of the following statements are facts taken from the reading. Other statements can be inferred from the reading. Write F in the blank in front of each factual statement. Write I in front of each inference.

_____ 1. Parasites are dangerous to the health of all creatures.

_____ 2. If a living creature can't clean itself, then some other animal has to do the job.

_____ 3. In a symbiotic relationship, both creatures benefit.

_____ 4. Even the simplest animals can adapt to situations when their lives depend on it.

_____ 5. Most of the animals whose job it is to clean others are fish.

_____ 6. Some fish actually change color while they are being cleaned.

_____ 7. A client fish will even go so far as to protect its cleaner fish, even when the client fish is put in danger.

_____ 8. Without cleaner fish, all fish would probably become extinct.

_____ 9. Even normally aggressive client fish will wait patiently for their turn with a cleaner fish.

_____ 10. A fish's survival instinct is stronger than its desire to eat the smaller cleaner fish.

Discussion

Discuss these questions with your classmates.
1. Discuss the cleanliness habits of other animals.
2. Discuss the relationship between cleanliness and health in humans and animals.
3. Discuss five ways in which our environment could be cleaned up.

Writing a Summary

Write a one-paragraph summary of Reading 1. Check your summary against the Summary Checklist on page 273.

Paraphrasing

Paraphrase paragraph 2 in Reading 2. Look at page 267–270 to find out about paraphrasing. Begin with either "According to Perry, . . . " or "Based on Perry's article, ..."

Research

Choose a particular concept (an abstract word) and define it in two or three ways in an extended definition such as the one in Reading 1. To gather information, you should consult a dictionary, look at related sources in the library, and/or draw on your own experience or that of your friends.

The following are suggested concepts:

Democracy	Love	Prejudice	Freedom
Patriotism	Fanaticism	Trust	Natural
Beauty	Education	Peace	Intelligence

You may use your research later to write a definition essay. The extended definition is discussed on pages 83–84.

Student Essay

Read the following essay written by a student.

Cleanliness

According to Webster's dictionary, the word *cleanliness* means "habitually kept clean." In fact, the quality, state, or condition of cleanliness is often determined by people's own culture, religion, occupation, or lifestyle. To comprehend the sense of cleanliness, each individual or culture has to be considered. In my country,

Japan, our basic sense of cleanliness may be more clearly defined by looking at basic aspects of our lives such as our buildings, our food, and hygiene.

Traditionally, it is the custom in Japan to keep our homes clean, since a clean house is a reflection of one's self. One way in which we keep our homes clean from outside dirt and germs is by taking off our shoes when entering our homes or even public places such as schools, local hospitals, and some restaurants. Upon entering a home, shoes are taken off and slippers are worn. Since shoes are taken off when entering someone's home, it is crucial that our socks be clean and have no holes in them. In the home, certain areas or rooms such as the bathroom or the yard require changing into different slippers which are used for that area. Also, our bathrooms are separated from our toilets, since the latter is considered to be a dirty place and therefore must be separate from the clean tub area. Needless to say, our floors are immaculately clean and must be scrubbed at least once a week.

When eating, there are other aspects of cleanliness that we consider. In a restaurant, clean chopsticks are provided just as clean silverware is provided in Western restaurants. However, it is difficult for a wooden chopstick to be kept really clean, so the Japanese discovered the disposable chopstick. Like most people, we wash our hands before eating, but in addition to this most restaurants provide diners with hot, steamed towels to clean their hands with before a meal. In the home, members of a family each have their individual chopsticks, rice bowl, and tea cup.

Being clean and hygienic is important to the Japanese. Westerners visiting Japan may see people wearing white gauze masks, like the ones used by surgeons, when they walk or bike through the city. People wear these because they may have hay fever or they may have a cold and do not wish to spread their germs to others or they may be afraid of air pollution. Also, when we have a cold we use paper tissues, which we throw away after use. We do not use a handkerchief to blow our noses with. Handkerchiefs are used for drying hands after washing or for wiping our mouths. It is considered good manners to always carry paper tissues with us wherever we go. Another custom we have when we come home from outside is to wash our hands with soap and water and rinse our mouths with water.

In conclusion, although the quality, state, or condition of cleanliness is determined by each individual, culture also plays a significant role. In Japan, there are general cultural norms with regard to cleanliness that most people follow in their daily lives. The main objective in every culture with regard to cleanliness is to keep people healthy.

Noriko
Japan

Student Essay Follow-Up

1. Underline the thesis statement.
2. Which three aspects of life in Japan does the writer focus on to define cleanliness?
3. Are all three aspects developed in the body paragraphs?
4. Examine paragraph 2. Do all the ideas support and illustrate the topic sentence?
5. Do you like the writer's definition of cleanliness? Explain your answer.

Organizing: Literal and Extended Definitions

Sometimes a definition appears in an essay to clarify a word. The definition may be expressed in a sentence or a paragraph, or it may even be the entire essay. The reason for this is that there are two kinds of definitions.

The first kind of definition gives the literal, or dictionary, meaning.

Example:

Cleanliness is the state of being free from dirt.

A literal definition is usually expressed in one sentence.

When you want to give a personal interpretation of a word, you use an extended definition. The extended definition may differ from the literal meaning because the word is defined in a particular or personal way. The meaning of an abstract word or concept such as "cleanliness" is often given in an extended definition, because such a word can be interpreted in different ways.

Example:

> In America, clean means not only free of dirt but free of odor as well.

The extended definition involves various kinds of supporting ideas. Reading 1 tells how the word *cleanliness* was defined by the Romans and the Greeks and in the Middle Ages. We are then given examples of similarities and differences in ideas of cleanliness among different cultures today.

In Reading 2, cleanliness is seen through the world of fish. We are given examples of how various species of cleaner fish and their clients go about the process of cleaning, and we are told of the importance of cleanliness to fish, without which many species would die.

Exercise 1

It is important to make your literal definitions accurate. Look at the definitions below. Which are accurate? Which are not? Rewrite the definitions that are not accurate.

1. Art is a mirror of the human soul.

2. Thermostats are devices that regulate heaters and cooling machines, turning them on and off so that they maintain the required temperature.

3. Wind means destruction from devastating storms or benefits from harnessing energy with windmills.

4. Powered flight is the realization of man's fondest dream over thousands of years.

5. A keynote address is an opening address that outlines the issues to be considered.

6. A mammal is a vertebrate animal with self-regulating body temperature and the capability for milk production by the female.

7. Mountain sickness is a sickness people get when they are in the mountains.

8. Separation anxiety is a negative emotional state that occurs in small children when they are parted from their parents.

9. Good sense is something everyone should hope to have.

10. Education is the key to prosperity.

Exercise 2

Work with a partner, a group, or alone. Look up the following words in a dictionary and write down their literal meanings. Then write three or four ways in which the definitions might be extended to include personal, social, or cultural meanings.

Example:

Touch   *Literal Meaning:*   to bring a bodily part in contact with something

        Extended Meaning: Different functions in society:
a. professional/functional
b. social/polite
c. to express friendship and warmth
d. to express love and intimacy

or   Different forms in different cultures:
a. North America
b. Latin America
c. Asia

or   Necessity for growth and development of certain animals:
a. monkeys
b. cats
c. dogs

1. Space   Literal Meaning: _____

                 Extended Meaning: _____

                 _____

2. Time

Literal Meaning: _____

Extended Meaning: _____

_____

3. Smell

Literal Meaning: _____

Extended Meaning: _____

_____

4. Aggressiveness

Literal Meaning: _____

Extended Meaning: _____

_____

5. Modesty

Literal Meaning: _____

Extended Meaning: _____

_____

6. Respect

Literal Meaning: _____

Extended Meaning: _____

_____

Introduction to the Definition Essay

In the introduction to a definition essay, state the term you are going to define. Then either define it yourself or use a dictionary definition, naming the dictionary and quoting from it. In your thesis statement, restate the term you are going to define and tell how you are going to define it, giving the three or four aspects from which you will illustrate your definition. Look back at the thesis statement of the student essay to see the three aspects of daily life the student used.

Using Etymologies

In your introduction, you may want to summarize the word's origin, or etymology. Look at pages 271–274 to find out about summarizing. Sometimes the original meaning of the word is quite different from its present meaning, and you may want to show this. The *Oxford English Dictionary* and many other unabridged dictionaries give detailed histories of the origin and development of words. For example, in *Webster's New Collegiate Dictionary,* we see that the word *boycott* comes from Charles Boycott, a land agent in Ireland who was ostracized for refusing to reduce rents; the word *prejudice* comes from the Latin *praejudicium,* which is made up of *prae,* meaning "before," and *judicium,* which means "judgment."

Using a Clear Definition

Many times a form of the word or the word itself is used as part of the dictionary definition, which does not make the meaning clear. For example, avoid defining cleanliness as "the state of being clean." Your definition will be clearer if you say, "Cleanliness is the state of being free from dirt."

Exercise 3

The following terms have been defined using a form of the term itself. Rewrite each definition without repeating the term being defined. Make sure the meaning of the word is clear.

1. fanaticism: fanatic outlook or behavior

2. loyalty: the quality or state of being loyal

3. education: the action or process of being educated

4. happiness: the state of being happy

5. creativity: the quality of being creative

6. friendship: the state of being friends

7. independence: the quality or state of being independent

8. leadership: the quality of a leader

Points to Remember in Organizing a Definition Essay

- Each body paragraph in your essay should illustrate an aspect of the definition that you stated in your thesis.
- Support each aspect with clear examples. (Look back at the student essay.)
- The conclusion should summarize your personal definition and give a final comment on the term.

Writing Practice

Choose one of the following topics.

1. Write a definition essay, using three or four examples, about one of the concepts you researched.
2. Write a definition essay on the concept of friendship. Illustrate your definition in three or four ways.
3. Write a definition essay on alcoholism.
4. Write a definition essay on respect, providing illustrations.

1. Pre-writing.

   Work alone, with a partner, or in a group.
   a. Brainstorm the topic. Look at page 258 to find out about brainstorming. Write down any mental associations you make with the word to be defined.
   b. Brainstorm for examples that can illustrate the word.
   c. Work on a thesis statement.

2. Develop an outline.

   a. Organize your ideas.
   Step 1: Write your thesis statement.
   Step 2: Select at least three examples that illustrate the term.
   Step 3: Read your examples over again to make sure they all define the term.
   b. Make a more detailed outline. The essay outline on page 22 will help you.

3. Write a rough draft.

4. Revise your rough draft.
   Use the Revision Checklist on page 262.

5. Edit your essay.
   Check your work for faulty shifts in person. If you start writing in the first person, you should not shift to second or third person within the same sentence.

   Example:

   Error: A person who exercises to avoid his or her problems is not necessarily reducing stress, especially if you have to go back to the same old problem the next day.

   Correct: A person who exercises to avoid his or her problems is not necessarily reducing stress, especially if he or she [or *the person*] has to go back to the same old problem the next day.

   Look at page 263 for symbols to use when editing your work.

6. Write your final copy.

Video Activity • Pedal Power

1. The video describes a washing machine that does not require electricity or running water. What are some places in the world where people would find this machine useful? Why?

2. Review the following words used in the video: *device* (noun), *portable* (adjective), *durable* (adjective), *refine* (verb).

3. After you watch the video, discuss the following questions.

   a. The speaker mentions "Gilligan's Island," a TV comedy in the United States about people who are shipwrecked on an uninhabited tropical island. Why might an invention like this appear on that show?

   b. Who invented the pedal-powered machine? Where was it invented?

   c. What kinds of materials were used to make the machine? How much does it cost?

   d. The machine is called "environmentally friendly." In what ways is it beneficial for the environment?

   e. How would you rate the machine in terms of creativity, cost, and energy efficiency?

4. How would you define the pedal-powered washing machine? Write a paragraph that defines it or some other pollution-free device for cleaning, like a broom, mop, or washboard. Follow this pattern:

   A _____ is a _____ that . . . .
   A *pedal-powered washing machine* is a *device* that . . . .

   Include several details about the device.

Internet Activity

- Use the Internet to find out about "ancient Roman baths." What were the bathing customs in ancient Rome? What were the different types of Roman baths? Where have ancient ruins of ancient Roman baths been discovered?

- What web sites did you use for your search? Which ones would you recommend to your class? Did you encounter any problems when searching for this information? How did you solve them?

CHAPTER FOUR

Groups, Organizations, and Societies

Pre-Reading Questions

Discuss these questions.

1. What groups or organizations can you name? Do you belong to any of these groups or organizations?

2. What are some organizations that are dedicated to doing good in the world?

3. Can you name some organizations that are harmful to society?

Activity

Read the following descriptions of some groups, organizations, and societies. Then find their names among those listed below.

Quakers	Masons	Mormons
The Amish	Big Brother	Scouts
Scientology	Salvation Army	Greenpeace
Red Cross		

1. This organization teaches young people to be good citizens and trains them to become leaders. Members are taught to do their duty to God, to their country, and to other people. Their mottos are "Be prepared" and "Learn by doing." The organization was started in Great Britain in 1907 by Robert Baden-Powell. Today, over five million Americans belong to this organization.

2. This group originated in Switzerland but is now centered in the United States and Canada. The largest communities are found in Ohio, Pennsylvania, Indiana, Iowa, and Illinois. This group believes in separation from the world. Members are forbidden to go to war, to swear oaths, or to hold public office. Their doctrine requires them to farm and to lead a simple life. The use of electricity and telephones is forbidden. Education is limited to the eighth grade.

3. This international organization calls attention to the environmental dangers of such actions as oil drilling, nuclear bomb testing, and dumping of radioactive wastes. The group also opposes whaling, the spread of nuclear weapons, and the inhumane killing of animals. Members use direct action and nonviolent methods of protest. They go where an activity that they consider harmful is occurring. Without using force, they try to stop the activity. The organization was founded in 1969 by a group of Canadians.

4. The men and women who belong to this organization devote their lives to helping people in need and spreading the Christian faith. The organization is supported by gifts of money from people who admire its work. This group is organized like an army. Its projects include providing medical care for the poor, inexpensive lodging for the homeless, and employment agencies to help people find jobs.

5. This is one of the oldest and largest fraternal organizations in the world. It is dedicated to the ideals of charity, equality, morality, and service to God. Members of this organization donate millions of dollars each year to charitable projects. The organization has millions of members worldwide, including three million in the United States. Membership in this organization is for males only. Recently, a similar organization was started for women. This is a secret organization; therefore, members will not say publicly that they belong to it.

Doctors Without Borders

Even in wealthy countries with technologically advanced health care systems, obtaining medical care can sometimes be difficult. Imagine being in a developing country where there is a war going on. There are no hospitals. There are no doctors. There is no medicine. You are injured and very sick. How can you get medical help?

In 1971, a group of doctors got together in France and created an organization called Médecins Sans Frontières, or MSF, which translates to Doctors Without Borders. These doctors believed that all people have the right to medical care, whatever their race, religion, or political affiliation, and that meeting their needs is more important than respecting national borders. The doctors wanted to give emergency aid to victims of war, epidemics, and disasters, whether natural or human in origin. To do this they organized volunteer teams of health care workers to go to often dangerous and remote areas.

At first, Doctors Without Borders was a very small organization. It consisted of volunteers who lived on money they earned from other jobs. Other international organizations considered the volunteers from Doctors Without Borders to be "amateurs" or "tourists." The organization did not grow very much because the volunteers did not ask for charity from the public for their service.

After 1978, because of world conflicts and the growth of refugee camps everywhere, the organization's activities spread like the roots of a tree. Doctors Without Borders began to take a more professional approach. It realized it needed funds and started to use the kinds of fund-raising techniques used in American political campaigns. This seemed to work well, and with the money it raised, Doctors Without Borders organized itself better and got better technology for dealing with emergencies. First, it began to pay an administrator and to give a small amount of money to doctors who were sent out for six months. Expanding from its origins in France, it developed sections in other countries—first in Belgium, Switzerland, the Netherlands, and Spain and later in other countries such as Australia and Canada. To encourage people to join the organization and give stability to its volunteers, it began to pay the doctors who worked in the headquarters, to give travel allowances, and to give a stipend of $700 a month to doctors who worked on long-term missions in the field. Since the 1980s, the number of doctors and nurses joining the organization has increased. In 1987, a U.S. branch of Doctors Without Borders was established in New York to allow American doctors to become involved. Having trained and worked in an organized and advanced medical system, American doctors wanted to see how big an impact their skills could have in a less developed country.

Doctors Without Borders is very efficient and quick to come to the aid of people in a crisis. However, before Doctors Without Borders decides it is needed in an area where there is a humanitarian crisis, it sends out an experienced team. The job of the team is to evaluate the medical and nutritional needs of the people in that area. The team looks at the transport and security facilities as well as the political environment. The team then sends its information to one of the operational offices. The Operations Department makes the final decision to intervene and starts the mission. People in this department decide who is going to be sent, the materials needed, and the medical priorities. Each mission is coordinated by one of the organization's sections. Then, within 24 hours, Doctors Without Borders sends emergency kits, which include generators and operating rooms that are the size of a conference table. These kits were developed by Doctors Without Borders and are used as models by emergency relief organizations worldwide. The kits are so complete that they can be used to provide medical assistance to thousands of people for several months. In 1991, within ten days of the departure of hundreds of thousands of Kurdish refugees from Iraq, Doctors Without Borders sent 75 airplanes loaded with 2,500 tons of equipment and supplies. After the kits are sent, teams of volunteers go to the crisis area and start their work.

Another of the missions of the organization is to bear witness and speak out. Doctors Without Borders is neutral and impartial as an organization and demands complete freedom in performing its job. However, sometimes medical help is not enough to save lives, and it is then that the organization will speak out to raise awareness so that some action can be taken. The point of speaking out is to improve conditions for the population in danger. In some situations, volunteers may give testimony at the United Nations, or they may openly criticize mass violations of human rights such as genocide, forced displacement of refugees, and war crimes. In 1994, Doctors Without Borders volunteers were among the peacekeepers sent to Bosnia. Volunteers witnessed great suffering. One doctor testified before the U.S. Congress about what he had learned: shots were fired at random into a group of some 230 people who were being kept in a small room, and then the dead and the injured were buried together. The testimony of the doctor led the United Nations to call these incidents "crimes against humanity."

Doctors Without Borders is independent and flexible in its operation because it is not funded by any government. Although the organization has its origins in France, it receives less than one percent of its total budget from the French government. It is a nonprofit organization that gets its funds from donations by the public. Some corporations, agencies, and other nonprofit organizations give financial support, too. Because it is not tied to government funding, it can maintain its independence and live up to its ideals.

In 1999, Doctors Without Borders won the Nobel Peace Prize for its "pioneering humanitarian work on several continents," in the words of the Norwegian Nobel Committee. One of the organization's founders, Bernard Koucher, said, "I'm deeply moved, and I'm thinking of all the people who died without aid, of all those who died waiting for someone to knock on their door." Since the organization was founded, volunteers have worked in Nicaragua, Afghanistan, Ethiopia, Rwanda, Kosovo, Timor, and Iraq, as well as with the Kurds.

Today, Doctors Without Borders has operations in more than 80 countries. These operations are run by more than 2,500 volunteer doctors, nurses, medical professionals, sanitation engineers, and administrators from 45 countries. These people work with 15,000 people who are hired locally to provide medical aid in troubled areas. Doctors Without Borders continues to find and to confront some of the greatest challenges in the world today.

Vocabulary

Select the letter of the answer that is closest in meaning to the italicized word or phrase.

1. Political *affiliation* does not matter to Doctors Without Borders.
   a. power
   b. association
   c. relatives
   d. problems

2. It realized it needed *funds.*
   a. money
   b. time
   c. advertising
   d. investments

3. The organization began to give its doctors a *stipend.*
   a. value
   b. loan
   c. salary
   d. credit

4. The stipend was for doctors who worked on long-term *missions.*
   a. conditions
   b. experiments
   c. research
   d. projects

5. Doctors Without Borders is *impartial.*
   a. has many parts
   b. treats all sides fairly
   c. does not reveal names
   d. does not take risks

6. Volunteers may *give testimony* at the United Nations.
   a. give evidence
   b. give their opinions
   c. talk about their lives
   d. write tests

7. Shots were fired *at random.*
   a. without a plan
   b. deliberately
   c. quickly
   d. one by one

8. It gets its funds from *donations* by the public.
   a. services
   b. contributions
   c. employment
   d. operations

9. Because Doctors Without Borders is not tied to a government, it can *live up to* its ideals.
   a. achieve
   b. solve
   c. investigate
   d. save

10. Doctors Without Borders continues to find and to *confront* some of the greatest challenges in the world today.
   a. avoid
   b. understand
   c. experience
   d. face

Vocabulary Extension

Part A

Match the parts of the following phrases as they were used in the context of the reading. Look back at the reading to check your answers.

1.	give emergency aid to	a.	emergencies
2.	take a	b.	victims of war
3.	deal with	c.	its ideals
4.	provide	d.	its independence
5.	maintain	e.	medical assistance
6.	live up to	f.	professional approach

Part B

Use each of the phrases in Part A to make a question about Doctors Without Borders. Start your questions with "What," Why," "Who," or "How."

Example:

How does Doctors Without Borders *maintain its independence*?

With a partner, take turns asking and answering the questions.

Comprehension

Looking for the Main Ideas

Some of the following statements from the reading are main ideas, and some are supporting statements. Write M in the blank in front of each main idea. Write S in front of each supporting statement.

_____ 1. In 1971, a group of doctors got together in France and created an organization called Médecins Sans Frontières, or MSF.

_____ 2. Other international organizations considered the volunteers from Doctors Without Borders to be "amateurs" or "tourists."

_____ 3. After 1978, with the growth of refugee camps everywhere, the organization's activities spread like the roots of a tree.

_____ 4. In 1987, a U.S. branch of Doctors Without Borders was established in New York to allow American doctors to become involved.

_____ 5. Doctors Without Borders is very efficient and quick to come to the aid of people in a crisis.

_____ 6. The team then sends its information to one of the operational offices.

_____ 7. Each mission is coordinated by one of the organization's sections.

_____ 8. Another of the missions of the organization is to bear witness and speak out.

_____ 9. In 1994, Doctors Without Borders volunteers were among the peacekeepers sent to Bosnia.

_____ 10. Since the organization was founded, volunteers have worked in Nicaragua, Afghanistan, Ethiopia, Rwanda, Kosovo, Timor, and Iraq, as well as with the Kurds.

Skimming and Scanning for Details

Scan the reading quickly to complete the following sentences.

1. Doctors Without Borders believes that all people have the right to medical care, whatever their _____, _____, or _____ _____.

2. Expanding from its origins in _____, the organization developed sections in other countries.

3. In 1987, a U.S. branch of Doctors Without Borders was established in _____ _____.

4. Volunteers sometimes give testimony at the _____ _____.

5. Doctors Without Borders is a _____ organization that gets its funds from donations by the public.

6. Today, the organization's operations are run by more than _____ volunteer doctors, nurses, medical professionals, sanitation engineers, and administrators.

7. Because Doctors Without Borders is not tied to government funding, it can live up to its _____.

8. Doctors Without Borders sends _____ _____, which include generators and operating rooms.

Making Inferences and Drawing Conclusions

Some of the following statements are facts taken from the reading. Other statements can be inferred from the reading. Write F in the blank in front of each factual statement. Write I in front of each inference.

_____ 1. Doctors Without Borders volunteers have witnessed great suffering and crimes against humanity.

_____ 2. Doctors Without Borders may speak out to raise awareness of a situation.

_____ 3. Doctors Without Borders is an organization that is similar to the Red Cross.

_____ 4. Doctors Without Borders sometimes gets to areas of crisis before other relief agencies.

_____ 5. Doctors Without Borders volunteers put their lives in danger when they volunteer.

_____ 6. Doctors Without Borders is a private, independent organization.

_____ 7. Doctors Without Borders gives emergency medical aid to people to whom other relief agencies will not give aid.

_____ 8. Doctors Without Borders has created unique emergency kits.

Discussion

Discuss these questions with your classmates.

1. Why do people volunteer to work for organizations like Doctors Without Borders?
2. What do you think Doctors Without Borders is doing that other relief organizations are not?
3. What are some other relief organizations and what do they do?
4. Do you think that these organizations should be funded by volunteers and private funds, or should governments take over this role?

Stranglers in a Strange Land

The following article, "Stranglers in a Strange Land" by Janet Milhomme, appeared in Escape Magazine *in 1994.*

Figure 1. 17th/18th century Indian Thugs. The Manson family of their day in India, called "Thags" in Hindustani, which means "deceivers." They traveled in gangs of up to 900 with one leader who directed all the moves and preyed on innocent travelers.

In the annals[1] of travel, there has never been a road hazard like them. Thugs were their name. Strangulation their game.

The Thugs, or Thugees as they were called then by the British, turned travel in 17th- and 18th-century India into a state of emergency. They murdered as many as 40,000 people a year for decades while authorities looked the other way and counted the protection profits.

Almost without exception, the Thugs preyed on travelers making their way along dusty Indian roads. They would insinuate themselves into the confidence of the travelers until the opportunity arose to strangle, rob and bury them. Master con men, they were called Thags in Hindustani, meaning "deceivers."

They were the Manson[2] family of their day and no traveler was safe from their wiles. To carry out the supposed wishes of the goddess Kali, cult[3] members, who numbered in the tens of thousands, staged elaborate productions to ensnare unsuspecting travelers. Each gang

---

[1]annals = historical records.

[2]the Manson family = a group, headed by Charles Manson, that committed some shocking murders in California in the 1960s.

[3]cult = a group of people who believe in a particular set of religious beliefs or principles, generally different from those of the majority.

(which might consist of as many as 900 men) had its leader who directed all the moves. Divided into separate parties of 10 to 20 persons, they either followed each other at a distance or, taking different routes, rendezvoused at appointed places, presumably by accident, and without appearing to know each other.

Thugs never acted without the strength of numbers or the element of surprise. Some of the gang were sent ahead to select a good killing site and dig graves while others brought up the rear to keep watch. If an advance party needed more assistance to kill their victims, they made certain marks on the roads, clues to the gang who followed that they were to hasten forward. So efficient was their system of communication that if travelers began to suspect one party, another group of Thugs would infiltrate. After getting rid of the first group, the second then strangled them. If travelers suspected or avoided both parties, two or more Thugs were ordered to keep them in sight, while signals were sent to other members in a production that might last a week or more before the victims were finally waylaid.[4]

Thugs traveled for days in the company of their prey, using every manner to gain their friendship and confidence, usually proposing that they travel together for safety reasons. The murders normally occurred when the party rested at an appropriate spot. The stranglers came up from behind with accomplices at their side. Two Thugs were considered indispensable and commonly three gave a hand.

Their weapon was a strip of twisted yellow or white silk knotted at one end with a silver coin consecrated to Kali. The Thug held the opposite end in his hand, and with a flick of the wrist, threw the weighted end around the victim's throat, and it was over in seconds. The bodies, dumped in shallow graves, were for Kali. Since Kali conveniently had no need for earthly treasures, the booty went to the Thugs.

Despite the mayhem,[5] there was no outcry from the authorities. Rajahs and Indian chiefs, corrupt police and petty local authorities offered protection for a price. It wasn't until Lord William Bentinck (British Governor-General of India, 1833–35) took steps to attack the system that the Thugees were seriously pursued. His chief agent was Captain William Sleeman, a young Bengal Army officer who led a 12-year campaign that finally broke up the Thugs through mass arrests and execution.

---

[4]waylaid = stopped from going wherever they were going.

[5]mayhem = chaos causing great damage.

From 1831 to 1837, 3,266 Thugs were captured, of whom 412 were hanged, 483 turned state's evidence,[6] and the rest were transported or imprisoned for life. Ironically, many of the arrests were achieved by exploiting the criminals' passionate devotion to family. Thugs turned themselves in after family members were captured and imprisoned, and to Sleeman's astonishment, they were not the brutes he had envisioned but in many cases were otherwise upstanding citizens and family men.

Their confessions, however, were stupefying[7]—many Thugs proudly admitting to an unthinkable number of murders. Their diaries, mostly lacking in detail, were monotonous lists of their morbid deeds.

"Left Poona and on arrival at Sarora murdered a traveler."

"On nearly reaching Bhopal, met 3 Brahmins and murdered them."

One Thug claimed to have strangled 431 persons during 40 years of Thuggee. He said there were many more, but he was so intent on luring them to destruction that he lost count.

For all those who thought the world was getting less safe, the Thugs provide a little perspective.

---

[6]to turn state's evidence = to give testimony for the government.

[7]stupefying = astonishing.

Vocabulary

Select the letter of the answer that is closest in meaning to the italicized word or phrase.

1. The Thugs *preyed on* travelers making their way along dusty Indian roads.
   - a. took as victims
   - b. traced
   - c. challenged
   - d. discovered

2. The Thugs *insinuated* themselves into the confidence of the traveler.
   - a. gradually suggested
   - b. completely concealed
   - c. highly advised
   - d. slowly introduced

3. Master *con men,* the Thugs were called Thags in Hindustani, meaning "deceivers."
   - a. learners
   - b. tricksters
   - c. thieves
   - d. instructors

4. No traveler was safe from their *wiles.*
   a. jokes
   b. stories
   c. tricks
   d. humor

5. Thugs staged elaborate productions to *ensnare* unsuspecting travelers.
   a. trap
   b. fight
   c. blame
   d. ruin

6. The Thug parties would give clues to the gang who followed that they were to *hasten* forward.
   a. approach
   b. volunteer
   c. shoot
   d. hurry

7. So efficient was their system of communication that if travelers began to suspect one party, another group of Thugs would *infiltrate.*
   a. run through
   b. go through
   c. blend in
   d. spread out

8. Their weapon had attached to it a silver coin *consecrated to* the goddess Kali.
   a. prepared for
   b. dedicated to
   c. chosen for
   d. equipped for

9. Since the goddess Kali conveniently had no need for earthly treasures, the *booty* went to the Thugs.
   a. gains
   b. medal
   c. award
   d. payment

10. To Sleeman's astonishment, the Thugs were not the *brutes* he had envisioned.
    a. strong characters
    b. unstable characters
    c. degraded characters
    d. weak characters

Vocabulary Extension

Part A

Read the list of verbs below. Find verbs in the reading that have the same meaning.

1. perform   <u>carry out</u>

2. go in advance   _____

3. eliminate   _____

4. help   _____

5. divide   _____

Part B

Make questions about the Thugs, using each of the verbs in Part A.

Example:

Why did the Thugs *carry out* these murders?

With a partner, take turns asking and answering questions.

Comprehension

Looking for the Main Ideas

Look at the reading to find the answers to the following questions.

1. What is the main idea of paragraph 5?

2. Which line states the main idea in paragraph 6?

3. Which sentence contains the main idea in paragraph 8?

Skimming and Scanning for Details

Scan the reading quickly to find the answers to the following questions. Write complete answers.

1. Whom did the Thugs murder?

2. Why did the Thugs murder people?

3. How many Thugs were there in India?

4. What did the Indian authorities do about the Thugs?

5. According to the reading, what would a group of Thugs do if travelers suspected their group?

6. According to the reading, why would a Thug travel with his victim?

7. When did the Thugs murder a party of victims?

8. What did they use to strangle their victims?

9. What does the word *system* in paragraph 8 refer to?

10. According to the reading, why were the Thugs' confessions stupefying?

Making Inferences and Drawing Conclusions

The answers to these questions are not directly stated in the reading. Circle the letter of the answer that best completes the sentence.

1. It can be inferred from the reading that Kali represented

   _____.

   a. wealth   c. destruction
   b. travel   d. power

2. From the reading, it can be inferred that the Thugs _____.
   a. were good actors   c. did not care about money
   b. worked alone   d. were outcasts of society

3. From the reading, it can be concluded that the Thugs _____.
   a. were a government organization
   b. were a widespread and powerful organization
   c. could be recognized easily
   d. were bothered by their conscience

Discussion

Discuss these questions with your classmates.
1. What are the pros and cons of belonging to an organized group?
2. Many people believe that crime today is worse than it was in the past. Argue for or against this statement.
3. If you belonged to a secret organization, could you keep its secrets all your life? If not, what do you think would happen?

Writing a Summary

Write a one-paragraph summary of Reading 1. Compare your summary to the Summary Checklist on page 273.

Paraphrasing

Paraphrase paragraph 5 in Reading 2. Look at pages 267–270 to find out about paraphrasing. Begin with either "According to Milhomme, . . ." or "Based on Milhomme's article, ..."

Research

Choose a particular group of people and find two or three dominant characteristics particular to them. Consult appropriate sources in the library, and/or use your own experience or that of your friends to gather information.

The following are suggested topics:

The Amish
The Shakers
Greenpeace
The Mormons
The Masons
The Salvation Army
The Boy Scouts/Girl Scouts
The Red Cross
The Quakers

Read the following essay written by a student.

Vegans

A vegetarian is someone who does not eat meat. However, there are many kinds of vegetarians. Some vegetarians don't eat meat, but they drink milk and eat cheese and eggs. Strict vegetarians are called Vegans. Vegans make an effort to avoid all forms of animal exploitation and live their lives accordingly. Most Vegans can be characterized by their avoidance of consuming animal foods and their derivatives, their avoidance of using products derived from animals, and their support for animal rights groups.

Vegans do not eat meat, fish, poultry, eggs or animals' milk and its derivatives such as yogurt, cheese, and butter. Vegans think it is cruel to make a cow produce milk all the time, and therefore they avoid any derivatives from milk. They avoid using gelatin, which comes from the bones of animals. Gelatin is used in many desserts; it is also used in photography, but Vegans have not found a substitute for this use yet. Most Vegans avoid eating honey because bees are often killed when they produce honey. As for eggs, chickens suffer as they are put in cages all their lives to lay eggs continuously. Vegans eat substitutes for these foods, which they can get in Vegan stores. These may be vitamins or derivatives from seaweed or soy.

Vegans avoid using any products derived from animals. For their clothes, they do not wear leather or fur. They also do not wear wool or silk. There are many ingredients from animals in many household items such as soap or shampoo. Vegans buy products that have the label "Cruelty Free" or "Not Tested on Animals." Even when they buy plates, they do not buy bone china because bone china really contains bones. There are Vegan stores where Vegans can buy foods and household items that are animal-free.

Most Vegans support animal rights groups. People who support animal rights believe that animals feel pain in the same way as humans do. Therefore, causing pain to an animal is the same as causing pain to a human. If animals have the same right to be free from pain and suffering as humans, then we can't eat them, take off their skins, experiment on them, or use them cruelly for our entertainment. These ideas are shared by most Vegans, who do not want to cause suffering to animals, and therefore many Vegans become supporters of animals rights.

In conclusion, Vegans can be generally characterized by their avoidance of consuming animal foods and their derivatives, their avoidance of using any products derived from animals, and their support for animal rights groups. However, this does not mean to say these are their only beliefs. Many Vegans have strong beliefs in human rights and the environment. Being a Vegan is a whole way of life.

Domenico
Ecuador

Student Essay Follow-Up

Before answering the following questions, read the following section on the dominant impression.

1. Underline the thesis statement.
2. What three characteristics of Vegans does the writer focus on?
3. Is each of these characteristics then developed in the body paragraphs?
4. Examine paragraph 2. Do all the ideas support the main idea? Are descriptive words used to strengthen the dominant impression?
5. Underline the dominant aspect or impression in each of the three body paragraphs.

Organizing: Description

Description is often used to make a narration or exposition more lively and interesting. An exposition may rely on some narration and description, and a narration may include some exposition and description. A descriptive essay, therefore, does not have to be purely descriptive but can use narration and exposition as well.

The Dominant Impression

A good description has two strong elements: a dominant impression and appropriate supporting details. The dominant impression is the main effect a place, an object, a person, or a group of people has on our feelings or senses. We create a dominant impression by selecting the most important characteristic or feature of the person or group of people or place and emphasizing that feature. We can then develop the dominant impression by providing details that support it.

In the student essay about Vegans, the three elements of the dominant impression are clearly stated in the thesis. They are then developed in the body paragraphs. The reading on Doctors Without Borders focuses on how the doctors put their beliefs into practice. The second paragraphs states, "These doctors believed that all people have the right to medical care, whatever their race, religion, or political affiliation, and that meeting their needs is more important than respecting national borders."

Examine paragraph 5 of the reading on Doctors Without Borders. How does it describe the organization's efficiency? Paragraph 6 describes how volunteers speak out about their beliefs. In what ways do they do this?

In the reading about the Thugs, the dominant impression that comes to mind is of their deceptiveness and their cold-bloodedness. Which paragraph clearly describes their cold-bloodedness?

Figures of Speech

Figures of speech are often used by writers to make their descriptions more vivid. Figures of speech are colorful words and expressions that make some kind of comparison. We will look at two figures of speech: the simile and the metaphor.

Simile

Of the many types of figures of speech, the simile provides the most direct comparison. In a simile, one thing is compared with another to show similarity, usually using the word *like* or *as*.

Examples:

The organization grew *like the roots of a tree.*
The Thugs were as efficient and well organized *as an army of ants.*

When writing similes, avoid very obvious and overused ones such as "easy as pie," "busy as a bee," and "he eats like a pig." Try to create your own fresh and interesting similes.

Complete the similes in the following sentences.

1. The Thugs were as cold-blooded as _____

_____ .

2. The Thugs preyed on their victims like _____

_____ .

3. The Thugs were as cunning as _____

_____ .

4. Captain William Sleeman was as courageous as _____

_____ .

5. The goddess Kali was as evil as _____

_____ .

6. The organization spread as quickly as _____

_____ .

7. The medical team is as efficient as a team of _____

_____ .

8. Their work is as desperately needed as _____

_____ .

Metaphor

A metaphor expresses a comparison more indirectly without using *like* or *as*. A word or phrase is used to suggest the strong likeness between the people or things being compared.

Examples:

Doctors Without Borders (The name is a metaphor comparing people to countries.)

They were the Manson family of their day. (The murderous activities of the Thugs are being compared to the horrible murders committed by the Manson family in the twentieth century.)

Exercise 2

Work with a partner or a group. Explain the comparisons being made in the following metaphors.

1. The Thugs were wolves in sheep's clothing.

2. They communicated with great efficiency; rarely did they miss each other's radar signals.

3. The roots of the organization spread into every country.

4. The Thugs were tigers in the grass, ready to pounce on unsuspecting victims.

5. Through their testimony, they hold a torch to the suffering of people everywhere.

6. Their knock on the door has saved the lives of many who had lost hope.

Writing Practice

Choose one of the following topics.

1. Write a descriptive essay using three dominant aspects of the group you researched earlier in this chapter.
2. Write a descriptive essay on an organization, a society, or a club that you are familiar with or would like to research. Use two or three adjectives to give the dominant impression.
3. Write a descriptive essay on a tribe or group of people that you are familiar with or would like to research. Use two or three adjectives to give the dominant impression.

4. Write a descriptive essay on a person you know. Use two or three adjectives to give the dominant impression.

1. **Pre-writing.**

   Work alone, with a partner, or in a group.

   a. Brainstorm the topic. Look at page 258 to find out about brainstorming. Choose a pre-writing technique you prefer.

   b. Brainstorm ideas for descriptive adjectives and supporting details.

   c. Work on a thesis statement.

2. **Develop an outline.**

   a. Organize your ideas.

      Step 1: Write your thesis statement.

      Step 2: Select two or three of the best descriptive adjectives from your brainstorming activity.

      Step 3: Find relevant descriptive details to support your dominant impression.

   b. Make a more detailed outline. The essay outline on page 22 will help you.

3. **Write a rough draft.**

   Look at page 261 to find out about writing a rough draft.

4. **Revise your rough draft.**

   Use the Revision Checklist on page 262.

5. **Edit your essay.**

   Check your work for the following type of error, known as a *dangling modifier.* The modifier *(visiting)* does not refer to the subject of the main clause.

   Example:

   Error: Visiting Pennsylvania some years ago, my friends told me about a group of people called the Amish.

   Correct: When I was visiting Pennsylvania some years ago, my friends told me about a group of people called the Amish.

   Look at page 263 for symbols to use when editing your work.

6. **Write your final copy.**

Video Activity • CITES Conference on Endangered Species

1. The video describes a meeting of CITES (Convention on International Trade in Endangered Species), the organization that regulates trade in endangered species of plants and animals. Why do you think this organization is necessary? What are some endangered species that need to be protected?

2. Review these words used in the video: *flora* (noun), *fauna* (noun), *poachers* (noun).

3. Watch the video once or twice and then do the following exercise. Check the correct answers.

   a. What endangered animal is not mentioned in the video?

      ＿＿ seahorse ＿＿ Bengal tiger ＿＿ elephant ＿＿ shark

   b. Bottled-nosed dolphins from the ＿＿＿＿＿＿ Sea will now be protected.

      ＿＿ Black ＿＿ Mediterranean ＿＿ Caribbean ＿＿ China

   c. Three southern African nations are now allowed to sell some ＿＿＿＿＿＿.

      ＿＿ gold ＿＿ ivory ＿＿ elephants ＿＿ birds

   d. Furniture makers from the United States opposed controls on the trade of ＿＿＿＿＿ from South America.

      ＿＿ oak ＿＿ ivory ＿＿ fabric ＿＿ mahogany

   e. The next CITES conference will be held in ＿＿＿＿＿.

      ＿＿ Japan ＿＿ France ＿＿ Thailand ＿＿ South Africa

4. Why is it so difficult to prevent poaching and other kinds of destruction of endangered species? Write a journal entry or short report about an endangered species from your country or region. What is being done to protect that animal or plant?

Internet Activity

- Use the Internet to find out about one of these organizations: UNICEF, Greenpeace, Friends of the Earth, WaterAid. Describe what the organization does. Does it provide volunteer opportunities in your area? If so, which ones would you like to participate in?

- Which web sites would you recommend to your classmates for finding volunteer opportunities in your city?

CHAPTER FIVE

Psychology

Pre-Reading Questions

Discuss these questions.

1. Look at the picture above of the muscular man. What do you think he is like? Place a check mark next to the adjectives that you think describe this man.

    ____ shy   ____ studious   ____ athletic
    ____ outgoing   ____ bold   ____ quiet
    ____ reserved   ____ imaginative   ____ tough-minded
    ____ sensitive

    Now look at the thin man. Place a check mark next to the adjectives that you think describe him.

    ____ passive   ____ talkative   ____ outgoing
    ____ intellectual   ____ thoughtful   ____ aggressive
    ____ easygoing   ____ calm   ____ active
    ____ anxious

2. On what basis did you characterize these people?
3. Is it possible that the thin man is outgoing and athletic and the muscular man is shy? Describe an incident in which you were wrong when you judged a person based on physical appearance.
4. Do people expect their leaders to look a certain way?

Body Language

"Let me have men about me that are fat," says Julius Caesar to Marcus Antonius in Shakespeare's play *Julius Caesar*. In Julius Caesar's opinion, fat people were more trustworthy than thin ones—that is, those with a "lean and hungry look," who "are dangerous."

Shakespeare wasn't the first person to categorize personality according to body type. And if you've ever reacted to people based on the way they look, you know he wasn't the last. The relationship between physical characteristics and personality has been explored for thousands of years and used to predict and explain the actions of others. Although prehistoric man probably had his own ideas about the skinny guy in the cave next door, the ancient Greeks historically have been responsible for Western theories about body and character.

The Greeks believed the body was composed of four humors, or fluids: blood, black bile, yellow bile, and phlegm. The one someone had the most of determined his or her temperament or personality type—sanguine (hopeful), melancholic (sad), choleric (hot-tempered), or phlegmatic (lazy or slow).

Although this ancient theory eventually lost its popularity, it was replaced over the next few thousand years by all kinds of other ways to identify and catalog people by type. One of the most popular modern theories was proposed by William Sheldon in the late 1940s and early 1950s. He suggested a relationship between body shape and temperament (see the figure). According to Sheldon's system, the endomorph, with an oval-shaped body and large, heavy stomach, is slow, sociable, emotional, forgiving, and relaxed. The mesomorph, with a triangular shape and a muscular, firm, upright body, is confident, energetic, dominant, enterprising, and at times hot-tempered. The ectomorph, with a thin, fragile body, is tense, awkward, and meticulous.

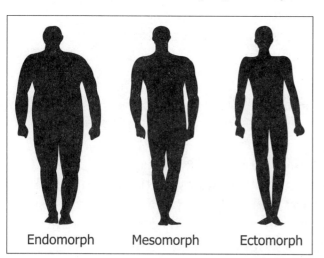

Endomorph   Mesomorph   Ectomorph

A number of researchers since Sheldon have contributed their own ideas to the basic theory that body shape and personality are somehow connected. Going one step beyond basic shape is the idea of "body splits." This theory looks at the body in sections—top to bottom, front to back, torso and limbs—with the idea that each part of the body tells its own story. For example, the upper half of the body, consisting of the chest, head, and arms, is expressive and conveys our feelings to others through gestures and facial movements. The lower body, on the other hand, is associated with more deeply felt emotions, particularly those about family, children, and self-image.

According to this theory, someone with a well-developed upper body will be active and outwardly confident. However, if this same person has noticeably thinner legs and narrow hips, he or she might have trouble expressing himself or herself to others, lack self-confidence, and find it difficult to think about deep emotions. A person with a small chest but large hips will have opposite traits, such as being shy in public but emotional and loving towards friends and family. Look for many clues to personality: weight distribution (heaviness or thinness in different parts of the body), muscular development, grace and coordination, and general health. For example, does one half of the body seem healthier, or more tense, or more relaxed than the other? Look for tense shoulders or stiff legs and hips.

Backs and fronts are different, too. The front of the body is associated with our conscious self, the one we think about and show to others. The back, which is hidden from us most of the time, is associated with our unconscious self—that is, the feelings we hide from both ourselves and others. Many times, we don't want to think about or show emotions such as anger and fear, and we tend to store these feelings in the back. If you're feeling stress, your back is likely to be tense. People who find it hard to deal with problems without losing their temper are likely to have some kind of back trouble. Look around you at the stories backs tell. A stooped back is weighed down by burdens or troubles. A stiff and rigid back is hiding anger or stress. A straight and graceful spine is strong and flexible. Do you know what kind of back you have?

Finally, there is the split between the torso, or body, and the limbs, or arms and legs. You express yourself with your arms and hands, and even your legs in the way you move about. People who are outgoing often use their hands and arms to gesture when they talk. They also walk with long, confident strides. Shy people hold their hands and arms quietly close to them and walk with small steps. Energetic people often tap their feet and move around a lot because it's hard for them to sit still. They can sometimes be impatient and are not the best listeners.

There is no end to theories about body shape and personality, and there is no doubt that certain people with certain bodies often have very predictable characters. However, there are some researchers who believe that the many instances in which body and personality go together are due to stereotyping; that is, we expect a certain type of person to have certain traits, so we see those traits whether they are there or not. For example, muscular people are believed to be dominant and forceful, so we treat them as leaders. But sometimes they are actually shy and timid. Fat people are supposed to be happy and warmhearted, but in reality they can just as easily be depressed or mean. Sometimes people will even act the way they think others expect them to act. By doing that, people fill the role in which we picture them.

No matter how you look at it, bodies and personalities are related, whether by chance or by choice. However, there are always exceptions to the rule, and whenever that happens, there goes the theory. After all, we're only human and that means we have a mind of our own— whether we're fat, skinny, or something in between.

Vocabulary

Select the letter of the answer that is closest in meaning to the italicized word or phrase.

1. According to Shakespeare's Julius Caesar, people with a "*lean* and hungry look" are dangerous.
   a. wild   c. weak
   b. thin   d. angry

2. The Greeks believed a choleric person was *hot-tempered*.
   a. lively   c. easily angered
   b. romantic   d. enthusiastic

3. The person with a triangular shape is confident, dominant, and *enterprising.*
    a. possessing the courage to start new and difficult things
    b. ready to attack at any time
    c. possessing special skills in business
    d. fond of being in control

4. The person with a thin, fragile body is tense and *awkward.*
    a. not friendly to people
    b. not very active or worried
    c. lacking in skill in moving his or her body
    d. lacking in ability to make decisions

5. The thin, fragile ectomorph is also *meticulous.*
    a. concerned about spending money
    b. concerned about details
    c. unable to decide
    d. unable to relax

6. Each section of the body—top to bottom, front to back, *torso* and limbs—tells its own story.
    a. the head and shoulders
    b. the front of the head and body
    c. the body without the head, legs, and arms
    d. the body with the head, but without the legs and arms

7. Look for clues to personality such as weight distribution, muscular development, *grace* and coordination, and general health.
    a. beauty and harmony in movement
    b. beauty of physical features
    c. healthy color of physical features
    d. straight and flexible body

8. A *stooped* back is weighed down by troubles.
    a. hardened
    b. painful
    c. tense
    d. bent

9. People who are outgoing walk with long, confident *strides.*
   a. movements   c. gestures
   b. steps   d. manners

10. Fat people can just as easily be depressed or *mean.*
    a. unkind   c. anxious
    b. moody   d. gloomy

Vocabulary Extension

Part A

Find words in the reading that go together with the words below to make phrases.

1. active and <u>confident</u>

2. burdens and _____

3. anger and _____

4. dominant and _____

5. shy and _____

6. happy and _____

Part B

Complete the sentences with the words you found in Part A.

1. A person who is _____ likes to talk a lot.

2. A _____ person is afraid of everything.

3. A _____ person is very generous.

4. A person who uses strength to get his or her own way is _____.

5. Someone with a stooped back usually has a lot of _____.

6. If you are under a lot of _____, you will get sick more often.

Part C

Do you agree with the definitions above? Make your own definitions, using the words you found in Part A.

Comprehension

Looking for the Main Ideas

Circle the letter of the best answer.

1. What is the main idea of paragraph 4?
   a. The Greek theory of personality lost its popularity over the years.
   b. Many personality theories had been developed by the 1940s and 1950s.
   c. William Sheldon's theory relates body shape to personality.
   d. Large, heavy people are usually sociable and emotional.

2. Paragraph 7 is mostly about
   a. the difference between a person's front and back.
   b. how stress and anger can cause back problems.
   c. how we hide our feelings from ourselves and others.
   d. what a person's back can reveal about him or her.

3. Paragraph 9 is mainly concerned with
   a. the many theories about body shape and personality.
   b. how stereotyping affects the way we see ourselves and others.
   c. how muscular people tend to be leaders.
   d. how some people have very predictable characters.

Skimming and Scanning for Details

Scan the reading quickly to find the answers to these questions. Write complete answers.

1. According to the reading, how has the relationship between physical characteristics and personality been used?

2. What are the four fluids and their related personality types, as defined by the Greeks?

3. What are the three shapes into which William Sheldon divided people?

4. In paragraph 5, sentence 1, to what does the word *their* refer?

5. In the theory of "body splits," what is the significance of the upper body?

6. In paragraph 6, line 1, to what do the words *this theory* refer?

7. What are four clues to personality that you should look for, according to the theory of "body splits"?

8. With which part of the personality is the front of the body associated?

9. According to the reading, what type of person may not be a good listener? Why?

10. What is the stereotype of fat people?

Making Inferences and Drawing Conclusions

The answers to these questions are not directly stated in the reading. Circle the letter of the best answer.

1. The reading implies that
   a. ancient people didn't know enough to understand personality theories.
   b. very few theories that categorize people by their appearance have been popular.
   c. it's natural for people to look for relationships between physical characteristics and personality.
   d. it takes a scientific mind to identify and categorize people according to body type.

2. From the reading, it can be concluded that
   a. our emotions and attitudes can affect our health and appearance.
   b. a person with a pleasant personality is most likely to be pear-shaped.
   c. the shape of the body as a whole tells the most about personality.
   d. it's easy to hide our emotions from others.

3. It can be inferred from the reading that
   a. people have lost interest in theories linking personality to looks.
   b. when we expect people to behave in a certain way, we're often disappointed.
   c. there is nothing to support theories about body shape and personality.
   d. stereotyping can make it difficult for us to see others as they really are.

4. The author's attitude toward theories that categorize people according to body type is
   a. disbelieving.   c. shocked.
   b. interested.   d. disappointed.

Discussion

Discuss these questions with your classmates.
1. Which physical characteristics do you use to categorize people?
2. What do you think of Sheldon's theory of relating body type to personality?
3. How can gestures and body movement be used to classify people?
4. Give some examples of how people are stereotyped.

Extraversion and Introversion

The following passage is taken from a college psychology text called
Personality *by Jerry Burger published by Wadsworth, a division of Thomson
Learning, Belmont, CA, 2000. In Chapter 9, The Biological Approach, Hans
Eysenck's theory of personality is described. Eysenck claims that differences in
personality are based on biological differences.*

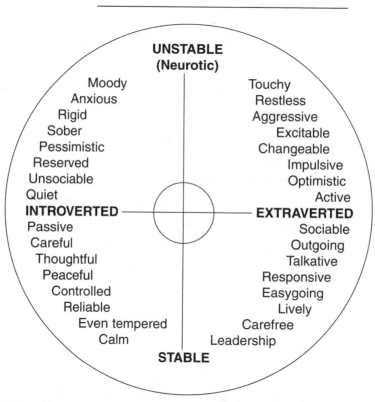

Figure 1. *Traits Associated with Eysenck's Two Major Personality Dimensions.*
Adapted from Eysenck and Eysenck (1968); reprinted by permission of
Educational and Industrial Testing Service.

Eysenck's research strategy begins by dividing the elements of
personality into various units that can be arranged hierarchically. The
basic structure in this scheme is the *specific response* level, which consists
of specific behaviors. For example, if we watch a man spend the
afternoon talking and laughing with friends, we would be observing a

specific response. If this man spends many afternoons each week having a good time with friends, we have evidence for the second level in Eysenck's model, a *habitual response.* But it is likely that this man doesn't limit himself to socializing just in the afternoon and just with these friends. Suppose this man also devotes a large part of his weekends and quite a few evenings to his social life. If you watch long enough, you might find that he lives for social gatherings, discussion groups, parties, and so on. You might conclude, in Eysenck's terms, that this person exhibits the *trait*[1] of sociability. Finally, Eysenck argues that traits such as sociability are part of a still larger dimension of personality. That is, people who are sociable also tend to be impulsive, active, lively, and excitable. All these traits combine to form the *supertrait* Eysenck calls **extraversion.**

How many of these supertraits are there? Originally, Eysenck's factor analytic research yielded evidence for two basic dimensions that could subsume[2] all other traits: *extraversion-introversion* and *neuroticism.* Because the dimensions are independent of one another, people who score on the extraversion end of the first dimension can score either high or low on the second dimension. Further, as shown in Figure 1, someone who scores high on extraversion and low on neuroticism possesses different traits than does a person who scores high on both extraversion and neuroticism.

Where do you suppose you fall in this model? If you are the prototypic[3] extravert, then Eysenck describes you as "outgoing, impulsive and uninhibited, having many social contacts and frequently taking part in group activities. The typical extravert is sociable, likes parties, has many friends, needs to have people to talk to, and does not like reading or studying by himself." An introvert is "a quiet, retiring sort of person, introspective, fond of books rather than people; he is reserved and distant except to intimate friends." Of course, most people fall somewhere between these two extremes, but each of us is perhaps a little more of one than the other.

Eysenck argues that extraverts and introverts differ not only in terms of behavior but also in their *physiological*[4] makeup. Eysenck originally maintained that extraverts and introverts have different

---

[1]trait = characteristic.

[2]subsume = include within its larger categories.

[3]prototypic = very typical; original after which others are modeled.

[4]physiological = biological; concerned with how the body works.

levels of *cerebral cortex arousal*[5] when in a nonstimulating, resting state. Although it may sound backward at first, he proposed that extraverts generally have a *lower* level of cortical arousal than do introverts. Extraverts seek out highly arousing social behavior *because* their cortical arousal is well below their desired level when doing nothing. In a sense, highly extraverted people are simply trying to avoid unpleasant boredom. Their problem is feeding their need for stimulation. Introverts have the opposite problem. They typically operate at an above-optimal cortical arousal[6] level. These people select solitude and nonstimulating environments in an effort to keep their already high arousal level from becoming too aversive. For these reasons, extraverts enjoy a noisy party that introverts can't wait to leave.

Unfortunately, a great deal of research has failed to uncover the different levels of base-rate cortical arousal[7] proposed by Eysenck. For example, introverts and extraverts show no differences in brain-wave activity when at rest or when asleep (Stelmack, 1990). But this does not mean that Eysenck's original theorizing was entirely off base. Rather, there is ample evidence that introverts are more sensitive to stimulation than extraverts are (Stelmack, 1990). That is, introverts are more quickly and strongly aroused when exposed to loud music or the stimulation found in an active social encounter. Introverts are even more responsive than extraverts when exposed to chemical stimulants, such as caffeine or nicotine.

Consequently, many researchers now describe extraverts and introverts in terms of their different sensitivity to stimulation, rather than the different base rate of cortical activity Eysenck proposed. However, the effect is essentially the same. Because of physiological differences, introverts are more quickly overwhelmed by the stimulation of a crowded social gathering, whereas extraverts are likely to find the same gathering rather pleasant. Extraverts are quickly bored by slow-moving movie plots and soft music because they are less likely to become aroused by these subtle sources of stimulation than introverts are.

---

[5]cerebral cortex arousal = level of activity in the part of the brain that is responsible for language, memory, and thinking.

[6]above-optimal cortical arousal = higher-than-desirable level of activity in the cerebral cortex.

[7]base-rate cortical arousal = low-degree activation of the brain.

Vocabulary

Select the letter of the answer that is closest in meaning to the italicized word or phrase.

1. Eysenck divided the elements of personality into units that can be arranged *hierarchically*.
    a. evenly
    b. randomly
    c. from higher to lower
    d. in groups

2. Traits are part of a larger *dimension* of personality.
    a. subject
    b. aspect
    c. division
    d. range

3. People who are sociable also tend to be *impulsive*.
    a. kind
    b. arrogant
    c. hasty
    d. cautious

4. Eysenck describes extraverts as "outgoing, impulsive and *uninhibited*."
    a. generous with money
    b. free and open
    c. unimaginative
    d. undependable

5. An introvert is "a quiet, *retiring* sort of person."
    a. possessing an excellent memory
    b. attending to duties willingly
    c. not fond of work
    d. tending to avoid the company of others

6. Eysenck thinks introverts are *introspective* and fond of books.
    a. thoughtful
    b. tolerant
    c. patient
    d. easygoing

7. Highly extraverted people try to feed their need for *stimulation*.
    a. excitement
    b. relaxation
    c. knowledge
    d. success

8. Introverts select nonstimulating environments in an effort to keep their already high arousal level from becoming too *aversive.*
   a. unimportant
   b. unpleasant
   c. unnecessary
   d. unsafe

9. There is *ample* evidence that introverts are more sensitive to stimulation than extraverts are.
   a. less than might be expected
   b. incomplete
   c. more than enough
   d. exactly enough

10. Extraverts are less likely to become aroused by *subtle* sources of stimulation than introverts are.
    a. hardly noticeable
    b. very unusual
    c. extremely displeasing
    d. constant

Vocabulary Extension

Part A

Read the list of verbs below. Find verbs in the reading that have the same meaning.

1. watch   *observe*

2. have or own   _____

3. claim   _____

4. suggest   _____

5. look for   _____

6. choose   _____

Part B

Complete the sentences with the words you found in Part A. Then look back at the reading to check your answers.

1. An extravert _____ different personality traits than an introvert does.

2. Extraverts tend to _____ noisy situations.

3. Introverts usually _____ solitude.

4. Eysenck _____ typical behavior of different personality types.

5. Eysenck _____ that people have different levels of cerebral cortex arousal.

6. Eysenck _____ a theory to explain the connection between cerebral cortex arousal and personality.

Part C

Now make a question using each of the verbs you found in Part A. With a partner, take turns asking and answering questions.

Part D

The phrases below can all be used to describe people. Make each adjective negative by filling in the blank with the most appropriate one of the following prefixes:

     ir   im   in   un

1. __offensive person
2. __flexible boss
3. __practical way
4. __discreet manner
5. __fallible judge of character
6. __efficient worker
7. __reproachable character
8. __rational thinker
9. __patient onlooker
10. __enlightened colleague
11. __sincere woman
12. __consistent behavior
13. __corruptible officer
14. __decisive child
15. __elegant posture
16. __judicious judgment
17. __responsible person
18. __personal judge
19. __bending father
20. __pretentious millionaire

Comprehension

Looking for the Main Ideas

Write complete answers to the following questions about the reading.

1. What is the main idea of paragraph 1?

2. Which lines state the main idea of paragraph 2?

3. What is paragraph 3 mostly about?

4. Which sentence contains the main idea of paragraph 4?

Skimming and Scanning for Details

Scan the reading quickly to complete the following sentences. Circle the letter of the best answer.

1. According to the reading, the basic structure in Eysenck's scheme for determining someone's personality type is _____.
   a. habitual response level
   b. supertraits
   c. specific response level
   d. extraversion

2. If a person often does the same activity, then that behavior is considered _____.
   a. not unusual
   b. trait
   c. a habitual response
   d. model behavior

3. According to the reading, a man who enjoys parties, gatherings, and discussion groups is exhibiting the trait of _____.
   a. sociability
   b. leadership
   c. optimism
   d. neuroticism

4. _____ is *not* an element of the supertrait "extraversion."
   a. Impulsiveness
   b. Activeness
   c. Liveliness
   d. Restlessness

5. Eysenck's original theory divided personality into _____.

    a.   three basic dimensions

    b.   several supertraits

    c.   impulsive and outgoing behavior

    d.   extraversion-introversion and neuroticism

6. According to Eysenck's theory, an introvert _____.

    a.   has many friends

    b.   likes books more than people

    c.   goes to parties several times a week

    d.   is impulsive

7. According to Eysenck, extraverts and introverts differ _____.

    a.   only in their behavior

    b.   both behaviorally and physiologically

    c.   only in their physiological makeup

    d.   mostly in the way they think

8. Eysenck was interested in comparing levels of cerebral cortex arousal in extraverts and introverts when _____.

    a.   they were resting

    b.   they were meeting other people

    c.   they were feeding their need for stimulation

    d.   they were alone

9. Eysenck thought that, compared to introverts, extraverts had _____.

    a.   a higher level of cortical arousal

    b.   nearly the same level of cortical arousal

    c.   a lower level of cortical arousal

    d.   a different kind of cortical arousal

10. According to Eysenck, extraverted people like busy, noisy places because _____.
    a. they're lonely without other people
    b. they're not very emotional
    c. they're shy
    d. they need the stimulation

Making Inferences and Drawing Conclusions

Some of the following statements can be inferred from the passage, and others cannot. Circle the number of each statement that can be inferred.

1. Eysenck didn't spend enough time studying people to come up with a good personality theory.

2. People who don't have many friends are unhappy.

3. You can't categorize a person according to his or her behavior in a single situation.

4. An extravert isn't easily embarrassed.

5. Introverts are more intelligent than extraverts.

6. An introvert would like a museum better than a crowded movie theater.

7. An extravert likes people more than he or she needs them.

8. An introvert's discomfort might be mistaken for unfriendliness.

9. It's difficult to categorize people because their personalities are too complex to fit into defined categories.

10. You are likely to find more extraverts than introverts at a packed, high-energy nightclub.

Discussion

Discuss these questions with your classmates.

1. Do you see yourself as an extravert or an introvert? Why?
2. Do you think Eysenck's theory makes sense? Why?
3. To what extent is personality hereditary? What other factors do you think affect the development of someone's personality?
4. Do you think people look for a partner whose personality type is like theirs? Do relationships between opposites work well?

Writing a Summary

Write a one-paragraph summary of Reading 1. Compare your summary to the Summary Checklist on page 273.

Paraphrasing

Paraphrase paragraph 4 in Reading 2. Look at pages 267–270 to find out about paraphrasing. Begin with either "According to Burger, . . . " or "Based on Burger's chapter, ..."

Research

Choose a particular subject that can be classified into three to five groups. Consult appropriate sources in the library, and/or use your own experience or that of your friends to gather information.
The following are suggested topics:

Socioeconomic groups	Blood groups	Personality types
Political groups	People's looks	Types of pollution
Types of TV shows	Types of wars	Types of emotions

You may use your research later to write your classification essay.

Student Essay

Read the following essay written by a student.

Classifying Personalities by Way of Astrology

The ancient Greek scientists observed the dazzling stars in the sky and created basic astronomy. They named each constellation after the characteristics of Greek gods. They used the twelve signs that appear in different periods in a year cycle to represent twelve human personalities. The twelve signs are Aries, Taurus, Gemini, Cancer, Leo, Virgo, Libra, Scorpio, Sagittarius, Capricorn, Aquarius, and Pisces. Each sign projects the character and personality of one specific Greek god. The person born under a certain sign has a personality related to the characteristics of that Greek god. These twelve astrological signs can be classified into the four elements in this world, which are wind, earth, fire, and water.

The three signs in the first category are Gemini, Libra, and Aquarius. The characteristics of this element are just like the name of the element, wind. The people in this category are natural-born debaters. Their skills allow them to have more advantages than others in their careers and enable them to overcome difficulties easily. A lot of people in this element are often important people in big companies. They are remarkable people compared to other groups. People in this category do not like steady jobs; they like work with challenges and prefer exciting jobs. Nobody knows what is going on inside their heads, just as you cannot catch the wind.

The second element, earth, includes the signs of Taurus, Virgo, and Capricorn. People born in this element have a rooted mind. They do not change their minds after making decisions. Their personality can be described as solid or immovable. Earth people usually exhibit a lot of patience. They can keep doing the same thing for years and often manage their lives into routines. Since they prefer doing stable tasks, they can often be found working for the government. These people are obstinate as stones but show higher loyalty to what they are doing than other groups. Earth people are often reliable partners in life.

Fire, the third element, includes the astrological signs of Aries, Leo, and Sagittarius. People born under this element tend to hurry and do not have a lot of patience. In the battle of their lives, they like to charge ahead and take their enemy's position. They also have a strong desire for success. Because of their personalities, they become leaders of groups. Also, since they are not afraid of taking risks, they often become pioneers in new fields such as explorers and inventors. Fire people are fighter types.

The last in the four elements is water, which includes the signs of Cancer, Scorpio, and Pisces. People in these three astrological signs have sensitive feelings in the areas of emotions and love. They are born with talent in the field of art. Many artists, poets, sculptors, and musicians belong to one of these three signs. They use their natural-born skills to create many delicate articles of brilliance unequaled by their contemporaries. The way they express themselves is as soft and tender as water. Water people often may be the closest friends or relatives in one's life. They are often perfect lovers, and there are many romantic stories about water people.

Classifying personality by using the four elements is not a foolproof method, and there are many exceptions. A person with the element water may have an impatient personality as in the element fire; a fire person may be interested in the field of art or music; a person in the element of wind may enjoy working in a steady job; and an earth person may have multiple lifestyles. Psychiatrists use many techniques to classify human personality. Although using astrological signs and the elements is a way of classifying human personality, there is not much evidence to support it since we have multiple personalities in general—but it is a fun way of classifying personality.

Hsing Chueh
Taiwan

Student Essay Follow-Up

1. Underline the thesis statement.
2. How does the writer classify astrological signs?
3. What signs are in the first category, and what are the characteristics of the first category? What signs are in the second category, and what are the characteristics of the second category? What signs are in the third group, and what are the characteristics of the third group? What signs are in the fourth group, and what are the characteristics of the fourth group?
4. Does the writer use supporting examples for each element?
5. Do all the members of your class fall under one of the elements?

Organizing: Classification

Classification means dividing people, objects, places, or ideas into various groups so that members of each group share similar characteristics. With this method, we give order to the many things in this world. Sociologists classify people into different classes; biologists classify plants or animals into species; and psychologists classify people's personalities into various types.

The Principle of Classification

In order to be clear, a classification should be based on a single principle. This means that you must choose one criterion on which to make your classification. In Reading 1 on body language, Sheldon classified people into three types—the endomorph, the mesomorph, and the ectomorph—based on the principle of body type. In Reading 2, Eysenck classified people into extraverts and introverts based on the principle of personality. In your classroom, you could classify the students according to their ethnicity: Hispanic, Asian, European. You could also classify the same students according to their age: under 20, between 20 and 25, over 25. Another classification of the same students could be according to their work in class: hard-working students, average students, lazy students. Yet another classification could be made based on where they sit in class: in the front rows, in the middle, in the back rows. As you can see, there are many principles that can be used; however, you must choose *one* principle of classification in your essay.

Once you have chosen a principle of classification, make sure that the classification includes all members of the group. For example, suppose you have decided to classify the students in your class by race. All the students fit nicely into the categories of Asian, Hispanic, and European, except for one who is Arabic and does not fit. You must either add another category so that this student will fit or look for another principle of classification.

To avoid omitting members, it is usually a good idea to divide the group into more than two categories. Most classification essays have three or four categories.

Exercise 1

Identify one item in each of the following groups and say how it is different from the others in that group. The first one is done for you.

1. Vehicles: car, truck, van, jeep, motorcycle.

   Motorcycle does not belong. All the others have four wheels.

2. Sports: football, baseball, tennis, volleyball, swimming.

3. Literature: poetry, newspaper article, short story, drama, novel.

4. Transportation: by land, by air, by sea, by bus.

5. Teachers: bachelor's degree, master's degree, Ph.D, brilliance.

6. Style of clothes: formal, semiformal, casual, beachwear.

7. Sports: hiking, skiing, swimming, ice-skating, tennis.

8. Animals: tortoise, crocodile, snake, lizard, monkey.

9. Food: protein, carbohydrates, fats, minerals, sugar.

10. Drugs: stimulants, depressants, hallucinogens, sedatives.

Look at the following subjects and categories. Identify the principle of classification being used. The first one is done for you.

1. Students: intelligent, average, below average

   Principle of classification: <u>level of intelligence</u>

2. Teachers: tough graders, fair graders, easy graders

   Principle of classification: _____

3. People: round faces, diamond-shaped faces, rectangular faces, square faces, triangular faces

   Principle of classification: _____

4. People: dark hair, blond hair, red hair

   Principle of classification: _____

5. Drivers: very careful, careful, careless, reckless

   Principle of classification: _____

6. Bats: plant eaters, blood eaters, fish eaters

   Principle of classification: _____

7. Burns: first-degree, second-degree, third-degree

   Principle of classification: _____

8. People: U.S. citizens, permanent legal residents, illegal residents

   Principle of classification: _____

Introduction in the Classification Essay

In your thesis statement, introduce the categories of classification you will be using.

Examples:

The students in my class can be classified according to their level of intelligence: those who are intelligent, those who are average, and those who are below average.

People can be classified according to the shape of their chin: those who have a pointed chin, those who have a round chin, those who have a broad chin, and those who have a small chin.

Wrinkles fall into two categories: horizontal and vertical.

Fish fall into three basic classes: jawless fish, bony fish, and cartilaginous fish.

When stating your categories in the thesis statement, remember to use parallel structure, or words of the same grammatical form, in the series.

Examples:

Teachers can be classified as *those who dress formally, those who dress semiformally,* and *those who dress casually.* (clauses)

In terms of body language, people can be classified according to *movements, posture,* and *facial expression.* (nouns)

The Greeks categorized people as *melancholic, phlegmatic, sanguine,* and *choleric.* (adjectives)

Transitions in the Classification Essay

For your classification essay, you will need several types of transitions:

1. Transitions that introduce categories:

the first	first	in addition
the next	second	finally
the last	third	besides

   Examples:

   The first group consists of students who are intelligent.
   The next category includes students who are average.

2. Transitions that show comparison and contrast:

unlike	in contrast to	while
whereas	different from	like

   Examples:

   Unlike the slow endomorph, the mesomorph is energetic.

   The temperament of the sanguine type, *in contrast to* that of the melancholic type, is hopeful.

3. Transitions that show examples:

one example	a good example	typical

   Examples:

   A good example of an extravert is the director of our company.
   Your tennis coach is a *typical* mesomorph.

Exercise 3

Fill in the blanks using the following transition words. Each word can be used only once.

next	besides	on the other hand
typical of	in addition to	last
whereas	a good example	fourth
third	first	

According to Dr. Li Tao in his book *How to Read Faces*, people can be divided into two broad categories: those who are mentally inclined and those who are firmly practical. Mind-oriented people have balanced faces that can be divided into three roughly equal sections. _____, physical types tend to have larger jaws and shorter faces. _____ these two broad categories, Dr. Tao divides faces into five basic shapes. The _____ is the round face with strong bone structure. It is _____ a mentally active person with self-confidence, resistance to illness, and a potentially long life. _____ is the diamond-shaped face, which indicates a generally warm, strong-willed, and lucky person. _____ is the rectangular face, and _____ is the square face. _____ the rectangular face indicates creativity, intelligence, and self-control, the square face belongs to an honest, well-balanced person with leadership qualities. _____ is the triangular face, with its wide forehead, prominent cheekbones, and pointed chin. _____ having a brilliant and sensual temperament, the triangular-faced person is intelligent and ambitious. _____ of such a person is the famous Elizabeth of Austria.

Writing Practice

Choose one of the following topics.
1. Write a classification essay, using three to five categories of classification, about one of the topics you researched in this chapter.
2. Write an essay about major types of food, using a principle of classification.
3. Write an essay classifying people by the way they dress. Establish your principle of classification and give examples of each group.
4. Write an essay classifying your friends into three or four major categories.

1. Pre-writing.

    Work alone, with a partner, or in a group.

    a. Brainstorm the topic. Look at page 258 to find out about brainstorming. Choose a pre-writing technique you prefer.

    b. Brainstorm for a principle of classification that includes all the members of the group. Do not have more than five categories, since you need to write a paragraph on each.

    c. Work on a thesis statement.

2. Develop an outline.

    a. Organize your ideas.
        Step 1: Write your thesis statement using parallel structure.
        Step 2: Identify each category, defining or describing it.
        Step 3: Give examples and specific details for each category.

    b. Make a more detailed outline. The essay outline on page 22 will help you.

3. Write a rough draft.

    Look at page 261 to find out about writing a rough draft.

4. Revise your draft.

    Use the Revision Checklist on page 262.

5. Edit your essay.

    Check your work for faulty parallel structures.

    Example:

    Error: There are three main skills a writer has to learn: to organize ideas correctly, logical thought, and clear expression of ideas.

    Correct: There are three main skills a writer has to learn: to organize ideas correctly, to think logically, and to express ideas clearly.

    Look at page 263 for editing symbols to use when editing your work.

6. Write your final copy.

Video Activity • Psychology Exhibit

1. The video describes an exhibit on psychology at the Smithsonian Institution in Washington, D.C. According to the video, science museums do not usually include exhibits about psychology. Why do you think this is so? Is psychology different from other sciences? If so, in what ways?

2. Review the following words in the video: *illusion* (noun), *diversity* (noun), *light-hearted* (adjective), *voyeurism* (noun).

3. After you watch the video, answer the following questions.

   a. How is this museum exhibit unusual?

   b. Describe three different displays in the exhibit. What do they look like and what do they demonstrate?

   c. What do children say about why they enjoy the exhibit? What do adults say?

4. Why do people go to museums? Do you think museums are necessary to society? Write a short journal entry describing why you like or dislike museums and saying how you think they might change in the future.

Internet Activity

- Find a "free personality test" on the Internet. What type of personality do you have, according to the test?

- Which web sites would you recommend to your class for finding out about personality theories?

CHAPTER SIX

Fashion in History

Pre-Reading Questions

Discuss these questions.

1. Describe this season's shoe fashions.
2. Why do fashions come and go?
3. Do you dress according to the latest fashions? Why or why not?

Activity

Our clothing and accessories send messages to others, which may be intentional or unintentional. Look at the six people in the photos below. Judging from their clothes and accessories, what can you say about their

1. economic status?
2. occupation?
3. nationality?
4. identification with a specific group?
5. likeableness?
6. age?

The Toe of the Shoe

There are no creatures on earth less practical than humans, and nothing shows our frivolity better than fashion. From women's hoop skirts[1] to men's high hats, fashion victims through the ages have endured the ridiculous, the uncomfortable, and the absolutely dangerous in an effort to be fashionable. Even our feet, which are normally planted firmly on the ground, have suffered the pains of keeping up with the latest craze.

Since shoes are meant to protect the feet, it's hard to believe that some styles have made walking nearly impossible. In ancient China, it was the custom to bind the feet of upper-class girls so that when they became women they could squeeze their stunted feet into silk shoes only four inches long. The binding process involved bending the toes under the feet, which were bound with tight wrappings worn day and night until the feet stopped growing. The girl's deformed "lily feet" left her capable only of being admired. In other words, she had to be waited on hand and foot.[2] In spite of the painful process, the girl considered the binding a great honor, as girls with "large" feet were often ridiculed.

According to legend, the practice started when a royal princess was born with very small, deformed feet. To save her from embarrassment in later years, it was decided that no lady of the court would be considered truly noble unless she had feet as tiny as the princess's. However the trend got started, Chinese poets helped it along by writing poems about the beauty of feet that were like "little golden lilies." A lady's tiny shoes and unsteady walk, if she could walk at all, were the pride of her wealthy husband, who saw that she was carried about and waited upon in the style to which she was accustomed. When a man chose a wife with "lily feet," he sometimes took a second wife to act as her servant.

---

[1]hoop skirt = a skirt containing a circle of flexible material that makes it stand out from the body.

[2]waited on hand and foot = constantly served or attended.

In the 1800s, the ruling Manchus passed a law forbidding the practice of foot-binding, but many families ignored the command and continued the ancient tradition. It wasn't until China became a republic in 1912 that the binding of a girl's feet was finally considered a criminal offense.

In contrast to China, in other parts of the ancient world men were usually the ones undergoing discomfort, as well as incredible inconvenience, because of their shoes. And in this case the problem was not feet or shoes that were too small, but rather oversized shoes, or at least shoe toes. Shoes with long, pointed toes were in fashion nearly 5,000 years ago in the Orient. The trend then spread to Asia Minor,[3] where the toe underwent one slight change to an upturned look. Eventually the fashion "turned up" in Egypt, Greece, and surrounding countries.

Some Egyptian rulers liked their five-inch shoe tips stuffed and formed in the shape of an uplifted elephant's trunk. Other Egyptian slippers spared no cloth with their eight-inch curled-up points. Although the toes were not quite as long, Greek and Roman magistrates[4] also wore shoes with turned-up toes as a symbol of their office when court was in session.

For more than 400 years, long-toed shoes went in and out of fashion, in a manner similar to the way hemlines[5] today fall below the calf[6] one year and touch the thigh the next. Long-toed shoes got a second chance in Europe when the Crusaders brought back samples of the style from Syria. By the 13th century, shoe tips were stretching out across Europe in all kinds of extravagant designs. Long-toed shoes characterized the man who didn't have to perform any physical labor, so the longer the toe, the wealthier the man. Imagine trying to work in a field while wearing shoes with foot-long toes!

Like well-watered weeds, long-toed shoes continued to grow until the 14th century, when some measured 30 inches from heel to toe. Toes alone extended up to a full foot beyond the human foot inside the shoe. Some toes turned out; some arched up and down like a miniature roller coaster;[7] others simply went outward and upward. To defy gravity, toes

---

[3]Asia Minor = Turkey.

[4]magistrates = officials who judge cases in the lowest courts.

[5]hemlines = lengths of skirts or dresses.

[6]calf = fleshy back part of the leg between the knee and the ankle.

[7]roller coaster = a kind of small railroad with sharp slopes and curves, popular in amusement parks.

were stuffed with moss,[8] hay, or wool and often stiffened with whalebone.

Long-toed shoes got so ridiculous that in the 1300s Pope Urban V and France's King Charles V condemned them as "an exaggeration against good manners" and "a worldly vanity." But these protests fell on deaf ears—or toes, in this case—because the wearing of long-toed, flip-flopping shoes only increased. In England, the toes were sometimes adorned with tiny silver bells, called "folly bells." Some shoes became so absurdly long that, to keep from tripping over them, the wearers held up the toes with fine chains attached to garters at their knees. So popular were long-toed shoes that the fashion continued through most of the 15th century and spread from nobles and wealthy people to other citizens, although many wore shoes with round and pointed toes of a more practical length.

Finally, long-toed shoes became such a nuisance that King Edward IV of England had laws enacted in 1463 to limit their length. But the laws didn't apply to everyone. In contrast to the privileged class, commoners were forbidden to wear shoes with toes more than two inches long. Any shoemaker who made shoes or boots that exceeded that limit was subject to a heavy fine. By 1470, French shoemakers were also forbidden to make shoes with long toes.

The fashion for long-toed shoes finally died out, but people couldn't seem to control their obsession with toes. In the early 1500s, in contrast to the previous century, toes went wide instead of long. The toes of some shoes were shaped in the form of a spread-open fan ten inches wide! Various styles had names like duck's bill, bear's paw, and cow's mouth. The silly-looking shoes invited mischief, and it's said that a favorite practical joke in both England and France was to come upon a gentleman unobserved and nail the broad toes of his shoe to the floor. Once again, like the long toe, the wide-toe style became so foolish and troublesome that a law was passed to limit toe width to six inches.

In comparison to the extreme width of men's shoes, women's shoes were only mildly wide. Their shoe fronts were frequently stuffed with hay or cloth and shaped into a series of giant toes. Sometimes they had grooves with linings of contrasting colors.

In 17th-century France, unlike previous eras, it was women who became the foot fashion leaders. They started a trend that has influenced ladies' footwear ever since. Small, tight-toed shoes were the

---

[8]moss = a small, flat, flowerless plant that grows like fur on wet soil or a wet surface.

French ladies' preference. They were so small, in fact, that some women, like the girls in ancient China, bound their feet with waxed linen tape so that they could squeeze them into the dainty shoes. So painful was this process that it was not uncommon for several of the queen's ladies to faint during court ceremonies because of the bindings.

A century later, American women still followed French fashion with tight, high-buttoned shoes with long, pointed toes. Although relief was at hand in the 1930s in the form of open-toed shoes, it wasn't long before ladies again were hobbling along in high-heeled, pointy-toed shoes, which continue to reappear every few seasons to torment women anew.

Why, one might ask, have men and women subjected their feet to silly, clumsy, cumbersome, painful, even dangerous footwear over the years? The answer, of course, is vanity. In spite of the fact that the first shoes were no doubt designed for protection, they eventually served as symbols of religion, wealth, rank, and social position. More than anything else, however, they have given their wearers a means of satisfying the human desire for adornment. Once the foot was enhanced with a bit of fur or a leather strap, appearance became more important than usefulness. Vanity went straight to man's feet, and we've been victims ever since.

Vocabulary

Select the letter of the answer that is closest in meaning to the italicized word or phrase.

1. Nothing shows our *frivolity* better than fashion.
   a. habits
   b. pride
   c. intelligence
   d. foolishness

2. Chinese women who had their feet bound as girls could squeeze their *stunted* feet into silk shoes only four inches long.
   a. undersized
   b. narrow
   c. fragile
   d. injured

3. To *defy* gravity, toes were stuffed with moss, hay, or wool.
   a. condemn
   b. delay
   c. control
   d. oppose

4. King Charles V condemned long-toed shoes as an example of "worldly *vanity.*"
   a. pretence
   b. disgrace
   c. pride
   d. imitation

5. Long-toed shoes became such a *nuisance* that King Edward IV had laws enacted to limit their length.
   a. amusement
   b. popular item
   c. inconvenience
   d. risk

6. In 17th-century France, unlike previous *eras,* it was women who became foot fashion leaders.
   a. time periods
   b. places
   c. special events
   d. groups of people

7. Some French women bound their feet with waxed linen tape so that they could squeeze them into the *dainty* shoes.
   a. highly decorative
   b. small and delicate
   c. embroidered
   d. sharp-pointed

8. High-heeled, pointy-toed shoes continue to reappear every few seasons to *torment* women anew.
   a. make proud
   b. cause pain to
   c. be unobtainable to
   d. improve the looks of

9. Why have men and women subjected their feet to *cumbersome* and even dangerous footwear over the years?
   a. useless
   b. foolish
   c. fashionable
   d. awkward

10. Shoes have given people a means of satisfying the human desire for *adornment.*
    a. approval
    b. decoration
    c. honor
    d. youthfulness

Vocabulary Extension

Part A

Read the list of words below. Find words in the reading that have the opposite meaning.

1. notice   _ignore_

2. obey   _____

3. allowed   _____

4. intelligent   _____

5. awkward   _____

6. survive   _____

Part B

Use the words you found in Part A to complete these questions.

1. What kinds of fashions nowadays are _____?

2. Why do some fashions quickly _____?

3. What fashions do you tend to _____?

4. What kind of clothing is _____ at your school or at work?

5. What kinds of school regulations do students often _____?

6. Do you mind looking fashionable but _____?

With a partner, take turns asking and answering these questions.

Part C

A compound adjective is often made by joining a past participle, or adjective ending in *ed,* to another word with a hyphen:

well-watered weeds (weeds that have a good supply of water)
high-buttoned shoes (shoes that are buttoned to the top)
high-heeled shoes (shoes that have high heels)

Adjectives with an *ed* ending can be made using words for parts of the body or parts of clothes.

eye: blue-eyed, dark-eyed
toe: long-toed, tight-toed
hair: long-haired, short-haired
heel: low-heeled, high-heeled

Change each italicized phrase into a compound adjective. The first one has been done for you.

1. A man *who has gray hair*   A gray-haired man

2. Shoes *that have rubber soles*   _____

3. Shoes *that have open toes*   _____

4. A shirt *that has long sleeves*   _____

5. A shoe *that has leather straps* _____

6. A shirt *that has an open neck*   _____

7. A man *who has wide shoulders*   _____

8. A girl *who has rosy cheeks*   _____

9. A pair of glasses *that has metal frames*   _____

Describe a person, using as many compound adjectives as you can.

Comprehension

Looking for the Main Ideas

Write complete answers to the following questions.

1. What is the main idea of paragraph 2?

2. Which line states the main idea of paragraph 7?

3. Which sentences contain the main idea of paragraph 13?

4. What is paragraph 15 mostly about?

Skimming and Scanning for Details

Scan the reading quickly to complete the following sentences. Circle the letter of the best answer.

1. According to the reading, the Chinese practice of binding a girl's feet began because _____.
   a. the poets encouraged it
   b. it made a girl more beautiful
   c. a royal princess was born with deformed feet
   d. it gave men an opportunity to take a second wife

2. In the Orient 5,000 years ago, the shoe fashion was _____.
   a. long, pointed toes   c. flat, wide toes
   b. upturned toes   d. toes with silver bells

3. Long-toed shoes were brought to Europe by _____.
   a. oriental traders   c. the Egyptian rulers
   b. the Crusaders   d. French aristocrats

4. In Europe, a long-toed shoe was a sign of _____.
   a. royalty   c. wealth
   b. poverty   d. vanity

5. _____ was *not* used to stuff long toes.
   a. Moss
   b. Newspaper
   c. Hay
   d. Wool

6. The laws enacted by Edward IV of England limiting the length of long-toed shoes applied mostly to _____.
   a. women
   b. the privileged classes
   c. shoemakers
   d. commoners

7. Shoes in the 1500s were very _____.
   a. practical
   b. silly-looking
   c. long
   d. heavy

8. In 17th-century France, ladies' shoes were _____.
   a. small, with very narrow toes
   b. very wide, with shoe fronts shaped into big toes
   c. open-toed and sandal-like
   d. high-buttoned

9. In the 18th century, American women _____.
   a. developed their own comfortable shoe style
   b. went back to the Greek style
   c. were influenced by French fashion
   d. began to bind their feet

10. The first shoes ever made were most likely designed for _____.
    a. adornment
    b. religious reasons
    c. attracting the opposite sex
    d. protection

Making Inferences and Drawing Conclusions

Some of the following statements can be inferred from the passage, and others cannot. Circle the number of each statement that can be inferred.

1. Fashion may be not only impractical but harmful as well.

2. Girls of ancient China either suffered the humiliation of having large feet or suffered the pain of having bound feet.

3. Some Chinese girls died because of the practice of foot-binding.

4. For some people, fashion is more important than comfort.

5. The Egyptian rulers didn't like the styles of the Orient.

6. What is silly or ugly in one era can be high fashion in another.

7. Thirteenth-century Europeans weren't open to new styles.

8. Throughout the ages, it has been women who have set the fashion trends.

9. Being fashionable has always been easier for the wealthy than for the common people.

10. Styles really haven't changed much over the years.

Discussion

Discuss these questions with your classmates.
1. What kinds of fashions have been or are physically harmful?
2. How do today's fashions show social or class distinctions?
3. What can you tell about a person from the clothing he or she wears?

Trousers and Skirts

The following reading is reprinted from Men and Women: Dressing the Part *by Claudia Kidwell and Valerie Steele (Smithsonian Institution Press, Washington, D.C., 1989), pages 13–15, by permission of the publisher. Copyright 1989. It compares and contrasts the wearing of trousers and skirts.*

How did modern Western men come to wear trousers and women skirts? As the history of dress evolved, two basic types of clothing developed. In warm countries, where weaving was invented more than 10,000 years ago, a draped or wrapped-and-tied style predominated (like the Roman toga, the Indonesian sarong, and the Indian sari). In cold countries, by contrast, nomadic people favored clothing made of animal skins cut and sewn together to follow the lines of the body (like the trousers and jackets of central Asian and northern European people). An intermediate type of clothing was the binary style, made of pieces of fabric sewn together and loosely following the lines of the body (like the Japanese kimono and the North African caftan). Binary clothes and wrapped garments could be folded flat, unlike the tailored clothes of the north, which fitted together with darts[1] and were three-dimensional. All three types entered the European tradition as a result of cultural contact, population movement, and invasion. The same thing happened in China.

But whereas in Europe, over the centuries, flowing robes became associated with femininity and tailored trousers with masculinity, this was not the case in China, where robes and trousers indicated not different gender, but different social status.

Trousers seem to have been invented in Persia in the later prehistoric period. They were then adopted by many northern European and central Asian "barbarians" (as they were referred to by "civilized" members of the Roman and Chinese empires), such as the Saxons. In many cases, barbarian women also wore trousers, especially when horseback riding was part of the nomadic way of life. In the cities of the two empires, however, both men and women of the elite wore long flowing robes (whether draped or binary). Even after the Roman Empire collapsed into a fragmented feudal Europe, noble men and women continued to wear long, quasi[2]-Roman robes. Peasants[3] wore short robes, and occasionally male peasants wore loose "barbarian" trousers.

Thus, the indigenous trouser tradition essentially died out in Europe—except in the clothing of soldiers. An aristocrat might wear a long robe at court, but he wore hose-like[4] trousers on the field of battle, often under his armor.[5] European men did not admire trousers, per se, but they did admire soldiers: the raison d'être[6] of the ruling aristocracy was its status as a warrior caste.[7] Women in Europe did not wear trousers because the garment had acquired such strong masculine connotations: what could be more masculine than a soldier?

In China, also, soldiers wore trousers (sometimes incorporated into suits of armor), but Chinese soldiers had no such exalted status, since

---

[1]darts = folds sewn into a garment to make it fit better.

[2]quasi = in some sense or degree.

[3]peasants = people who worked on the land in former times.

[4]hose-like = looking like stockings.

[5]armor = strong protective metal covering worn in battle by fighting men.

[6]raison d'être = reason or justification for existence.

[7]warrior caste = social class made up of soldiers.

the Chinese masculine ideal was the scholar-bureaucrat,[8] who wore a robe. In China, peasants of both sexes wore trousers, so there was a basic division between rulers in robes, on the one hand, and peasants and soldiers in trousers on the other. Women could and did wear trousers. Even upper-class Chinese ladies (and gentlemen) wore trousers for horseback riding or on less formal occasions.

Back in medieval Europe, aristocratic men gradually developed a new, high-fashion type of trousers. First, however, they shortened their robes. Not that they adopted the coarse short robes of peasants; rather they developed elaborate and very short robes worn over tight stockings. Eventually, this new robe turned into a doublet,[9] and the top of the stockings into short, puffy bloomers[10] which turned into knee breeches.[11] At the end of the eighteenth century, knee breeches merged with plebian[12] long trousers to become modern men's pants. Women continued to wear long skirts—very long skirts for high-born women and their middle-class followers, and shorter skirts for peasants and working-class women.

The Victorians opposed female trousers and short skirts, not so much because they were prudish about female legs, but because they vehemently rejected clothing with mixed gender and class messages. Women could wear bifurcated[13] garments only under special conditions: at fancy dress parties (Turkish trousers were popular), sometimes for hunting, as part of bathing dress, and eventually as underpants. A few peasant and pioneer women wore trousers, as did some women who worked in mines.

Trousers [for women] were only very gradually accepted after World War I. But in the 1920s, "Conspicuous Outrage"[14] began to become as much a part of fashion as "Conspicuous Consumption." Even so, we forget how restricted most trouser-wearing really was during the Jazz Age.[15] Trousers were acceptable in the form of beach pajamas, lounge wear, riding jodhpurs,[16] and eventually blue jeans. But it was

---

[8]bureaucrat = a person who works for the government.

[9]doublet = a close-fitting jacket worn by European men in earlier times.

[10]bloomers = loose trousers gathered at the knee.

[11]knee breeches = short, more fitted trousers fastened at the knee.

[12]plebian = of the common people.

[13]bifurcated = split in two.

[14]outrage = offense against accepted standards of behavior or taste.

[15]Jazz Age = period between World War I and 1929.

[16]riding jodhpurs = pants worn when riding horses.

only in the 1940s and 1950s that casual trouser-wearing became common among teenagers, college coeds, and suburban housewives ("a little blue denim number for Eve to garden in . . ."). Trousers were still unacceptable as urban street wear or for work. As late as 1960, *Harper's Bazaar* ran an advertisement showing a woman, first in a black shirtwaist dress and again in a white (bifurcated) jumpsuit,[17] with the caption: "First we stole his shirt . . . now we steal his overall" indicating that both the button-down shirt and trousers were still regarded as masculine articles of clothing, no matter how long women had worn them.

_____

[17]jumpsuit = a one-piece garment consisting of a blouse attached to trousers or shorts.

Vocabulary

Look at the reading to answer the following questions.

1. What does the word *elite* in paragraph 3 mean?
   - a. upper class
   - b. scholars
   - c. people who travel
   - d. political candidates

2. Which word in paragraph 4 means "native"?

3. What is another way of saying *per se*?
   - a. in order
   - b. all things considered
   - c. as such
   - d. in truth

4. Which of the following could substitute for *connotations* in paragraph 4?
   - a. differences
   - b. associations
   - c. complications
   - d. similarities

5. Which of these statements is true?
   - a. An *exalted* status is at a lower level.
   - b. *Exaggerated* means the same as *exalted*.
   - c. Something *exalted* is honored.
   - d. *Exalted* means common.

6. Which word is closest in meaning to *coarse* in paragraph 6?

    a. poor quality   c. highly decorated

    b. of superior kind   d. square in shape

7. Which word in paragraph 7 means "shy and proper"?

8. What is another word for *vehemently*?

    a. quietly   c. humorously

    b. politely   d. strongly

9. Which word in paragraph 8 is similar in meaning to *noticeable*?

10. What does the word *coeds* in paragraph 8 mean?

    a. fashionable women   c. male and female students

    b. female students   d. graduate students

Vocabulary Extension

Part A

Match the adjectives with nouns as they were used in the context of the reading. Look back at the reading to check your answers. Add two more nouns that may be used with each adjective.

    a. clothes   c. street wear   e. status

    b. connotations   d. consumption   f. way of life

1. _e_ social   status   _____   _____

2. ___ tailored   _____   _____   _____

3. ___ nomadic   _____   _____   _____

4. ___ masculine   _____   _____   _____

5. ___ conspicuous   _____   _____   _____

6. ___ unacceptable   _____   _____   _____

Part B

Use the adjectives and nouns you listed in Part A to complete these sentences about clothing fashions. Then look back at the reading to check your answers.

1. In Europe, wearing trousers had strong _____ _____.

2. In China, robes and trousers indicated _____ _____.

3. People in the north wore close-fitting _____ _____.

4. Horseback riding was part of the _____ _____.

5. _____ _____ in the 1920s included buying luxury fashion items.

6. Trousers were _____ _____ for women until the 1960s.

Part C

Now make new sentences using the adjective and noun combinations you chose in Part A.

Comprehension

Looking for the Main Ideas

Some of the following statements from the reading are main ideas, and some are supporting statements. Find the statements in the reading. Write M in the blank in front of each main idea. Write S in front of each supporting statement.

_____ 1. As the history of dress evolved, two basic types of clothing developed.

_____ 2. In cold countries, by contrast, nomadic people favored clothing made of animal skins cut and sewn together to follow the lines of the body (like the trousers and jackets of central Asian and northern European people).

_____ 3. Binary clothes and wrapped garments could be folded flat, unlike the tailored clothes of the north, which fitted together with darts and were three-dimensional.

_____ 4. Peasants wore short robes, and occasionally male peasants wore loose "barbarian" trousers.

_____ 5. Thus, the indigenous trouser tradition essentially died out in Europe—except in the clothing of soldiers.

_____ 6. Back in medieval Europe, aristocratic men gradually developed a new, high-fashion type of trousers.

_____ 7. Eventually, this new robe turned into a doublet, and the top of the stockings into short, puffy bloomers, which turned into knee breeches.

_____ 8. Trousers for women were only very gradually accepted after World War I.

_____ 9. Trousers were acceptable in the form of beach pajamas, lounge wear, riding jodhpurs, and eventually blue jeans.

_____ 10. Trousers were still unacceptable as urban street wear or for work.

Skimming and Scanning for Details

Scan the reading to complete the following sentences.

1. In warm countries, the early form of dress was a _____ style, such as the Roman _____, the Indonesian _____, and the Indian _____.

2. Clothing in the _____ style is made from pieces of fabric sewn together and loosely following the lines of the body.

3. The three early styles of dress from various parts of the world became incorporated into European tradition as a result of _____, _____, and _____.

4. In China, robes and trousers indicated a difference not in gender but in _____ _____.

5. Trousers are believed to have been invented in _____ in the _____ time period.

6. Members of the Roman and Chinese empires considered themselves civilized compared to the people of northern Europe, whom they called _____.

7. In the Roman Empire, the peasants wore _____ robes while the nobility wore _____ robes.

8. In medieval Europe, trousers were something the _____ wore, and therefore they became associated with _____.

9. The Victorians were opposed to having females wear either _____ or _____, because they preferred styles that gave a clear message regarding _____ and _____.

10. In the 1940s and 1950s, trousers became popular among _____, _____, and _____.

Making Inferences and Drawing Conclusions

Some of the following statements are facts taken from the reading. Other statements can be inferred from the reading. Write F in the blank in front of each factual statement. Write I in front of each inference.

_____ 1. Climate and geography have influenced the evolution of clothing styles.

_____ 2. The Japanese and the North Africans had similar clothing styles.

_____ 3. Although flowing robes were worn by both male and female Europeans in early times, this style of dress eventually became associated with femininity.

_____ 4. In nomadic societies for whom horseback riding was a way of life, women often wore trousers.

_____ 5. It is likely that the peasants' clothing was made more practical than the clothing of noblemen so that it wouldn't interfere with their work; the noblemen didn't have to go out and build things and plow fields.

_____ 6. Unlike the Europeans, the Chinese valued intellect over brute force.

_____ 7. Aristocratic women of medieval Europe wore long skirts, while the peasant women wore shorter skirts.

_____ 8. Victorian women were repressed by strict social codes.

_____ 9. Even in the 1950s, trousers were not acceptable attire for the working woman.

_____ 10. No matter how modernized society becomes, it is still difficult to break from traditional social ideas.

Discussion

Discuss these questions with your classmates.

1. What do you consider to be a masculine look for men and a feminine look for women?
2. Do you think men and women should dress alike? Why or why not?
3. Fashionwise, which period would you like to have lived in? Why?
4. How important are clothing fashions to civilization?

Writing a Summary

Write a one-paragraph summary of Reading 1. Check your summary against the Summary Checklist on page 273.

Paraphrasing

Paraphrase paragraph 5 of Reading 2. Look at pages 258–260 to find out about paraphrasing. Begin paraphrasing with either "According to Kidwell and Steele, . . ." or "Based on Kidwell and Steele's research, ..."

Research

Choose two styles and find three points of comparison and contrast between them. Consult appropriate sources in the library, and/or use your own experience or that of friends to gather information.

The following are suggested topics:

Two styles of architecture
Two periods in fashion
Forms or styles of housing in two different countries
Two styles of furniture
Clothing styles in two different countries
Two cars

You may use your research later to write a compare-and-contrast essay.

Student Essay

Read the following essay written by a student.

Short Skirts of the Twenties and Sixties

Fashion always adjusts to periods and tells the truth about an age without benefit of hindsight. Many of the social changes of the 20th century are reflected in the changes of fashion. The decades of the "Swinging Sixties" and the "Roaring Twenties" were the fun periods of the century, conveying the lighter side of life. They are also remembered as the decades of short skirts. In this essay, the rise and fall of short skirts and other features of fashion of the Twenties and Sixties will be compared and contrasted in relation to social changes and economic and political conditions.

Electro-technological advances after World War I, like the refrigerator and vacuum cleaner, encouraged more women to work outside the home, and a degree of female emancipation progressed. The new mass media such as movies, the radio, and records captured more audiences than ever and sped up the standardization of society. Such social development forced the style of women's clothes to become simpler and more practical so that women could lead active lives. Consequently, in the mid-1920s, the real revolution of short skirts began. In the Sixties, there was a social development similar to that of the Twenties. The wave of female emancipation, which affected women's clothes, was irreversible. The new mass medium, TV, was well installed in Europe and the United States, and music and dancing influenced women's clothes through TV. More advanced female emancipation and electro-technology in the Sixties made women's skirt lengths shorter than in the Twenties. Short skirts in the Twenties were just above the knee; on the other hand, the young women of the Sixties exposed the greater part of their thighs. Thus, short skirts came into fashion.

In both the Twenties and the Sixties, a new accepted type of beauty was the unisex type; that is, girls strove to look as much like boys as possible. French women, who had had the initiative in fashion for a long time, were too feminine and differed much from the unisex type. This time, it was England and the United States that were the initiators of fashion rather than Paris. For the unisex look, short skirts went well with short hair. Women's hair fashion in the Twenties was the shingle; that is, the top of the head was flat and the sides softer, straight or curly. The shingle became one of the most significant symbols of women's liberation in the Twenties. Compared with the hair fashion of the Twenties, the Sixties had a diversity of hair fashions. The most famous hair fashion was the Vidal Sassoon haircut. It was cleverly shaped by layering to an even overall length, and it was easy to manage and keep.

The fall of short skirts was influenced by economic and political conditions. Skirts suddenly became long again as the decade of the Twenties drew to its close. In the United States, the Wall Street Crash in October 1929 triggered the slump and the Great Depression. Also, in Europe, the rise of Hitler began. The focus on legs had lost its appeal, so another one had to be found. With the fall of short skirts in the Twenties, the emphasis shifted from legs to the back. Instead of bare legs, women had backs bared to the waist. On the other hand, at the end of the Sixties, the fashion never shifted from its focus on legs. But while young women exposed their legs, they began to expose their tops in see-through blouses. As the decade of the Seventies began, the age of the mini-skirt ended, giving rise to the longer midi-skirt. This change in fashion was influenced by the oil crisis and distrust of politics like Watergate and Vietnam in the Seventies.

It is said that fashion repeats itself every 30 or 40 years. According to this theory, the mini-skirts of the Sixties came into fashion almost 40 years after the short skirts of the Twenties. Short skirts in both decades were accompanied by similar social changes, and the political and economic conditions in both decades affected their fall. Although these fun decades have gone into the past, they still sparkle in history. Fashion is always a mirror of the period.

Nubia
Peru

Student Essay Follow-Up

1. Underline the thesis statement.
2. From what point of view will the fashions of the Twenties and Sixties be compared and contrasted?
3. In paragraph 2, what conditions were similar for women in the Twenties and Sixties?
4. What is the similarity discussed in paragraph 3?
5. What influenced the end of short skirts in the Twenties and Seventies?
6. Underline the topic sentences in paragraphs 3 and 4 that show comparison (similarity).

Organizing: Comparison and Contrast

Comparison and contrast is a very useful and common method of essay organization. Many college essay assignments require you to compare and contrast ideas, theories, facts, characters, principles, and so on. In your personal life, too, you find similarities and differences in a whole array of things, from the products you buy to the friends you make and the jobs you get.

When you *compare* two items, you show how aspects of one item are similar to aspects of another. A comparison tells you what features are *similar*.

When you *contrast* two items, you show the differences between them. You point out the features that are not alike or are *different*.

Finding Two Comparable Items

In order to make a comparison, you need to choose two items that share a similar feature or have the same function. In Reading 1, the toes of shoes were compared in different periods; in the student essay, short skirts of the Twenties were compared with short skirts of the Sixties. It would not be a good idea to compare the clothes of a rich woman with the uniform of a nurse. However, two kinds of uniforms could be compared and contrasted.

Exercise 1

Work with a partner. Write the names of two examples for each group. Say why the examples could be compared.

1. fast food restaurants: _____ _____

2. amusement parks: _____ _____

3. computers: _____ _____

4. cars: _____ _____

Basis of Comparison

The basis of comparison is an important aspect of the organization and development of a comparison-and-contrast essay. When comparing two items, you must compare the same aspects of each. For example, in comparing two people, the basis of comparison could be appearance, behavior, or personality. Whatever bases of comparison you choose, you must use the same ones to discuss each person. You cannot compare the personality of one person to the appearance of the other.

As an example, here are some of the possible bases for comparing two universities:

Bases of Comparison	University A	University B
size	large	small
location	rural	urban
reputation	affordable	expensive
specialty	engineering	the arts

Thesis Statement

In a comparison-and-contrast essay, you may want to compare and contrast two items to show that one is better than the other, that the two are totally different, or that they have some similarities and some differences. Purposes will vary.

The thesis statement for a comparison-and-contrast essay should include the names of the two items being compared and the dominant impression of each item.

Example:

University A is a better choice for me than University B because of its size, location, reputation, and specialty.

1. Write a thesis statement for an essay in which you compare two fast food restaurants.
2. Write a thesis statement in which you compare two kinds of cars.

Organizing a Comparison-and-Contrast Essay

There are two basic ways to organize a comparison-and-contrast essay: (1) block organization and (2) point-by-point organization.

In block organization, one item, such as University A, is discussed in one block (one or more paragraphs), and the other is discussed in another block. In Reading 1, small feet were discussed in one block, and then oversized shoes were discussed in another. In Reading 2, the European association of flowing robes with femininity and trousers with masculinity was discussed in one block, and then what these garments were associated with in China was discussed in another block.

In point-by-point organization, similarities and differences on the same point are discussed together.

Imagine you were going to write a comparison-and-contrast essay about the clothing styles in Los Angeles and New York City. The following outlines show how you might organize your essay using either the block or the point-by-point approach.

Block Organization Outline

Topic: A Comparison and Contrast of the Clothing Styles in Los Angeles and New York City

Thesis Statement: The clothing style in Los Angeles is quite different from that of New York City in terms of fabrics, colors, and style.

I. Los Angeles
   A. Fabrics (light, same for summer and winter)
   B. Colors (bright)
   C. Style (casual)
II. New York City
   A. Fabrics (heavy, different for summer and winter)
   B. Colors (not bright)
   C. Style (formal)

Conclusion

Point-by-Point Organization Outline

Topic: A Comparison and Contrast of the Clothing Styles in Los Angeles and New York City

Thesis Statement: The clothing style in Los Angeles is quite different from that of New York City from the point of view of fabrics, colors, and style.

I. Fabrics
   A. Los Angeles (light, same for summer and winter)
   B. New York City (heavy, different for summer and winter)
II. Colors
   A. Los Angeles (bright)
   B. New York City (not bright)
III. Style
   A. Los Angeles (casual)
   B. New York City (formal)

Conclusion

As you can see, the block organization is simpler because fewer transitions are required and one subject is discussed completely before going on to the other. The point-by-point organization, in which similarities and differences of each point are discussed together, requires repeated use of comparison-and-contrast indicators.

Comparison and Contrast Indicators

A good comparison-and-contrast essay is sprinkled with comparison and contrast indicators, or structure words. The following is a list of some of these structure words.

Comparison Indicators

Sentence Connectors	Clause Connectors	Others
similarly	as	like (+ noun)
likewise	just as	similar to (+ noun)
also	and	just like (+ noun)
		(be) similar to
		(be) the same as
		both . . . and
		not only . . . but also

Underline all the comparison indicators in Reading 1 and Reading 2.

Contrast Indicators

Sentence Connectors	Clause Connectors	Others
however	although	
nevertheless	even though	but
in contrast	while	yet
on the other hand	whereas	despite (+ noun)
on the contrary		in spite of (+ noun)

Underline all the contrast indicators in Reading 1 and Reading 2.

Join the two sentences using the comparison or contrast word indicated. Make any necessary changes. The first one is done for you.

1. *although*

   In China, foot-binding was a painful process for girls. Girls considered it a great honor.

   <u>Although foot-binding was a painful process for girls in China, they considered it a great honor.</u>

2. *whereas*

   In China, women experienced inconvenience over shoes. In other parts of the world, men experienced inconvenience over shoes.

3. *likewise*

   The long-toed shoe became foolish and ridiculous. The wide-toed shoe became foolish and ridiculous.

4. *just as*

   A law was passed to limit shoe-toe length. A law was passed to limit shoe-toe width.

5. *however*

   Women wore moderately wide shoes. Men went to extremes with the fashion.

6. *In contrast*

   In Europe, robes were associated with femininity. In China, robes were associated with social status.

7. *whereas*

   In China, rulers wore robes. Peasants and soldiers wore trousers.

8. *while*

   At the end of the 18th century, high-born and middle-class women wore long skirts. Peasant and working-class women wore shorter skirts.

9. *just as*

   The fashion of short skirts ended in the 1920s because of troubled economic and political conditions. Short skirts went out of fashion in the 1970s because of troubled economic and political conditions.

Writing Practice

Choose one of the following topics.

1. Write a comparison-and-contrast essay, using three points of comparison and contrast, about one of the topics you researched in this chapter.
2. Write a comparison-and-contrast essay about two people you know or know something about. Use three or four bases of comparison.
3. Write an essay about a place you know, comparing and contrasting the way it was at some time in the past to the way it is now.
4. Compare and contrast two groups of people in your native country. Compare their lifestyles, social status, and feelings toward each other.

1. **Pre-writing.**

   Work alone, with a partner, or in a group.

   a. Brainstorm the topic. Look at page 258 to find out about brainstorming. Choose a pre-writing technique you prefer.
   b. Brainstorm for your bases of comparison and supporting ideas.
   c. Work on a thesis statement.

2. **Develop an outline.**

   a. Organize your ideas.

   Step 1: Write your thesis statement.
   Step 2: Select three or four bases of comparison from your brainstorming activity.
   Step 3: Find relevant supporting details for each point.

    b.   Make a more detailed outline. Choose between the block and point-by-point organization outlines on page 172.

3. Write a rough draft.

        Look at page 261 to find out about writing a rough draft.

4. Revise your draft.

        Use the Revision Checklist on page 262.

5. Edit your essay.

        Check your work for faulty shifts in time. These happen when you change tense within a sentence or paragraph for no significant reason.

Example:

Error: In warm countries, people wore loose clothing made from cotton or linen. In cold countries, they prefer clothing made from animal skins.

Correct: In warm countries, people wore loose clothing made from cotton or linen. In cold countries, they preferred clothing made from animal skins.

        Look at page 263 for symbols to use when editing your work.

6. Write your final copy.

Video Activity • Shoes and Fashion

1. The video describes a show in France where new and unusual shoe designs are displayed. Why do people wear uncomfortable shoes or clothes? Are people in the modern era as fashion-conscious as those who lived in earlier periods?

2. Review the following words used in the video: *well-heeled* (adjective), *bridle* (noun), *rip off* (verb), *exotic* (adjective).

3. After you watch the video, read the questions and put a check before the correct answer(s).

   a. The reporter in the video wears shoes that look like _____.

      ____ hands   ____ feet   ____ flowers   ____ boots

   b. The reporter says, "Beauty is in the eye of the beholder." This proverb means that

      ____ the eyes are the most beautiful feature people have.
      ____ beauty comes from inside.
      ____ people have different perceptions about what is beautiful.
      ____ we see what we want to see.

   c. The design of one pair of Clare Singleton's shoes was inspired by _____.

      ____ the night sky   ____ bridles   ____ duck feet   ____ platforms

   d. About _____ designers are hired each year by well-established companies.

      ____ 10   ____ 15   ____ 20   ____ 25

   e. The last designer interviewed in the video uses exotic products like _____ and _____ in her shoes. (Choose two.)

      ____ diamonds   ____ fish skin   ____ amethysts   ____ ivory

Internet Activity

- Use the Internet to find out about these famous designers: Christian Dior, Coco Chanel, Rei Kawakubo, Manolo Blahnik. What kind of clothing or accessories is each of them specially noted for?

- Which web sites would you recommend to your class for finding out about the latest clothing fashions?

Nutrition

INGREDIENTS: CRUST: ENRICHED FLOUR (FLOUR, NIACIN, FERROUS SULFATE, THIAMINE MONONITRATE, RIBOFLAVIN), WATER, HYDROGENATED SOYBEAN OIL, CONTAINS LESS THAN 2% OF THE FOLLOWING: DRY YEAST, SOY FLOUR, SALT, BAKING POWDER (MONOCALCIUM PHOSPHATE, BAKING SODA), DEXTROSE, SORBITAN MONOSTEARATE. **TOPPINGS:** COOKED PORK SAUSAGE (PORK, SALT, SPICE, NATURAL FLAVOR), MOZZARELLA AND PASTEURIZED PROCESS AMERICAN CHEESE SUBSTITUTES (MADE FROM WATER, CASEIN, HYDROGENATED SOYBEAN OIL, MALTODEXTRIN. CONTAINS LESS THAN 2% OF THE FOLLOWING: SODIUM ALUMINUM PHOSPHATE, SALT, LACTIC ACID, SODIUM CITRATE, SODIUM PHOSPHATE, ARTIFICIAL COLOR, SORBIC ACID (PRESERVATIVE), CITRIC ACID, ZINC OXIDE, FERRIC ORTHOPHOSPHATE, VITAMIN A PALMITATE, RIBOFLAVIN, FOLIC ACID, MAGNESIUM OXIDE, VITAMIN B6 HYDROCHLORIDE, NIACIN, THIAMINE MONONITRATE), PEPPERONI (PORK, MECHANICALLY SEPARATED PORK, BEEF, SALT, WATER, DEXTROSE, SPICE AND COLORING, LACTIC ACID STARTER CULTURE, GARLIC POWDER, SODIUM NITRITE, BHA AND BHT AND CITRIC ACID ADDED TO PROTECT FLAVOR, SMOKE FLAVOR. MAY ALSO CONTAIN BEEF STOCK), GREEN PEPPERS, ONIONS, COOK CHEESE (SKIM MILK, CHEESE CULTURE, CALCIUM CHLORIDE, ENZYMES), TEXTURED VEGETABLE PROTEIN (SOY FLOUR, CARAMEL COLOR), HYDROGENATED SOYBEAN OIL. **SAUCE:** TOMATO PUREE (WATER, TOMATO PASTE), WATER, SUGAR, MODIFIED CORN STARCH, SALT, SPICE, HYDROGENATED SOYBEAN OIL, BEET POWDER, XANTHAN GUM, NATURAL FLAVOR, ARTIFICIAL COLOR.

Pre-Reading Questions

Discuss these questions.

1. Why do products have labels?
2. Do you know why it is important to read the labels on products?
3. Do people use additives in food in your country?
4. How long do you think additives have been used in food?

Activity

Match the labels to the products.

1.

MADE WITH WATER, ENRICHED FLOUR (BARLEY
MALT, NIACIN, IRON (FERROUS SULFATE) THIAMIN
MONONITRATE, RIBOFLAVIN), HIGH FRUCTOSE CORN
SYRUP, WHEAT GLUTEN, SOY FIBER, COTTONSEED FIBER,
CONTAINS 2% OR LESS OF: YEAST, CALCIUM SULFATE,
SALT, CORN BRAN, FLAVORS (NATURAL), SOY FLOUR,
CORN GRITS, ETHOXYLATED MONO- AND DIGLYCERIDES,
CELLULOSE GUM, MALTODEXTRIN, SODIUM STEAROYL
LACTYLATE, MONO- AND DIGLYCERIDES, YEAST
NUTRIENTS (AMMONIUM SULFATE), STARCH, VINEGAR,
SOY PROTEIN, PRESERVATIVES (CALCIUM PROPIONATE).

2.

CURED WITH WATER, HONEY, POTASSIUM LACTATE, SALT,
CARRAGEENAN, DEXTROSE, SODIUM PHOSPHATE,
SODIUM ERYTHROBATE, SODIUM NITRATE.

3.

INGREDIENTS: WATER, CANOLA OIL, PARTIALLY
HYDROGENATED CORN OIL, MALTODEXTRIN, SALT,
VEGETABLE MONOGLYCERIDES (EMULSIFIER), POTASSIUM
SORBATE AND CALCIUM DISODIUM EDTA AND CITRIC
ACID TO PRESERVE FRESHNESS, ARTIFICIAL FLAVOR,
COLORED WITH BETA CAROTENE (SOURCE OF VITAMIN
A), VITAMIN A PALMITATE AND VITAMIN D$_3$ ADDED.

4.

INGREDIENTS: WATER, CORN SYRUP, LIQUID SOYBEAN
OIL, MODIFIED FOOD STARCH, EGG WHITES, VINEGAR,
MALTODEXTRIN, SALT, NATURAL FLAVORS, GUMS
(CELLULOSE GELL AND XANTHAN GUM), ARTIFICIAL
COLORS, SODIUM BENZOATE AND CALCIUM DISODIUM
EDTA USED TO PROTECT QUALITY.

The Story on Food Additives

What's that on your pizza? You can bet it's not just the extra cheese and onions you ordered. As a matter of fact, you can count on at least a dozen other "extras" that you never asked for, including dextrin, mono- and diglycerides, potassium bromate, sodium aluminum phosphate, sodium citrate, sodium metabisulfate, and xanthan gum. These common food additives make your pizza, among other things, lighter, tastier, and generally more pleasing to the palate. Because we like our pepperoni[1] without mold, our crackers crispy, our peanut butter smooth, and our tomatoes red, chemicals are added to just about everything we eat. They make food more flavorful and easier to prepare; they make it last longer, look more appetizing, and feel better in our mouths (no lumps!).

Today's additives read like a chemistry book, so many people believe they're a modern invention. However, additives are nothing new, and neither is the controversy surrounding them. London in the 18th century could have been called the "adulterated[2] food capital of the world," though it's likely that other cities in other countries were just as guilty of the practice of food adulteration. One might think that food in the "old days" was pure and simple, but in many cases, what people paid for was not what they were getting. Pepper, for example, was adulterated with mustard husks,[3] pea flour, fruit berries, and sweepings from the storeroom floor. Tea, which was very expensive and brought all the way from China, was mixed with dried leaves from ash trees.[4] China tea was green, so fake China tea was often made from dried thorn leaves[5] colored with a poisonous substance called verdigris. When black Indian tea became popular, it was common for manufacturers to buy up used tea leaves, which they stiffened with a gum solution and then tinted with lead, another dangerous substance.

[1]pepperoni = a very spicy pork or beef sausage often put on pizzas.

[2]adulterated = made impure or of poorer quality by adding other substances.

[3]mustard husks = the dry outer coverings of mustard seeds.

[4]ash trees = trees belonging to the olive family.

[5]thorn leaves = the dry, hard, pointed leaves from thorn bushes.

Even candy was contaminated with highly poisonous salts of copper and lead to give it color. These practices eventually came to the public's attention, and in 1860 the first British Food and Drug Act was passed. Despite the regulations on food purity that currently exist in almost every country, there are still problems. One of the most alarming cases occurred in 1969 when an Italian gentleman was charged for selling what was supposed to be grated parmesan[6] cheese but turned out to consist of grated umbrella handles!

Believe it or not, food adulteration is not all bad. Salt has been used as a preservative for thousands of years, and, thanks to some basic and other quite complicated substances, we have "fresh" vegetables in January, peanut butter that doesn't stick to the roof of the mouth, stackable potato chips, and meat that doesn't turn green on the way home from the grocery store. But as they say, there's a price to pay for everything.

In the case of vegetables and fruits, the price is taste. Bred[7] for looks and long hauls,[8] plump, red tomatoes have fine body and perfect skin but offer very little for our taste buds[9] to smile about. The reason is that the tomatoes are picked green and then "gassed" along the way; that is, they're treated with ethylene gas, the same gas tomatoes give off internally if allowed to ripen on the vine.[10] The artificial gassing tricks the tomatoes into turning red. They don't really ripen; they just turn a ripe color.

The federal government recognizes about 35 different categories of additives, which are used for various purposes. Antioxidants are added to oil-containing foods to prevent the oil from spoiling. Chelating agents stop food from discoloring. Emulsifiers keep oil and water mixed together. Flavor enhancers improve the natural flavor of food. Thickening agents absorb some of the water present in food and make food thicker. They also keep oils, water, and solids well mixed. About 800 million pounds of additives are added to our food every year.

What happens when we consume this conglomeration of chemicals? The average American ingests about five pounds of food additives per year. The good news is that the majority of the hundreds

---

[6]parmesan = a hard, dry, strong-flavored cheese that is often sold grated.

[7]bred = produced by selecting parent plants with certain characteristics.

[8]long hauls = transportation over long distances.

[9]taste buds = small groups of receptor cells on the tongue that distinguish different tastes.

[10]the vine = the plant.

of chemicals that are added to food are safe. In some cases, they're even good for us, such as when vitamins are added. The bad news is that some of them are not safe, and these are the ones with which we need to concern ourselves.

The first of the unsafe additives is artificial sweeteners. The sugar substitute aspartame is sold commercially as Equal or NutraSweet and is used in many diet beverages.[11] However, studies have shown that about one out of 20,000 babies cannot metabolize one of the two substances that aspartame is made from and that toxic levels of that substance, called phenylalanine, can result in mental retardation.[12] Some scientists also believe that aspartame can cause problems with brain function and behavior changes in people who consume it. Some people who have consumed aspartame have reported dizziness, headaches, and even seizures.[13] Another controversy over aspartame involves its possible link to an increased risk of brain tumors. Aspartame is still widely added, although many lawsuits have been filed to block its use. Another sugar substitute called saccharin has been linked to cancer in laboratory animals.

The additives sodium nitrite and sodium nitrate are two closely related chemicals that have been used for centuries to preserve meat. These additives keep meat's red color, enhance its flavor, and stop the growth of dangerous bacteria. Nitrate by itself is harmless, but it is quickly changed into nitrite by a chemical reaction that occurs at high temperatures and may also occur to some degree in the stomach. During this chemical reaction, nitrite combines with other chemicals to form some very powerful cancer-causing agents. Bacon is a special problem because it is thinly sliced and fried at a high temperature. Other processed meats, such as hot dogs, ham, and bologna, are less of a risk. Nitrite has been considered an important cause of stomach cancer in the United States, Japan, and other countries. In the United States, in fact, the rate of stomach cancer has been declining for a number of years because of reduced use of nitrite and nitrate preservatives.

Artificial colorings, often used in combination with artificial flavorings, replace natural ingredients that are more costly to produce.

---

[11]beverages = drinks other than water, alcohol, or medicine—for example, coffee and tea.

[12]mental retardation = underdevelopment of mental ability.

[13]seizures = sudden or violent attacks, such as those associated with epilepsy.

Lemon-flavored "lemonade" is much cheaper to make than a real lemon product. Artificial colorings are synthetic dyes such as Blue No. 1, Blue No. 2, Citrus Red No. 2, Green No. 3, Red No. 3, Red No. 40, Yellow No. 5, and Yellow No. 6. They are widely used in foods to make them look more natural and more attractive. All those colored breakfast cereals for kids are loaded with food dyes, as are ice cream, cakes, and other tasty treats. For decades, questions have been asked about the safety of synthetic food dyes, and many dyes have been banned for being toxic or cancer-causing. There are still questions of safety about the dyes that are currently in use. Yellow No. 5, for example, causes allergic reactions in some people. Red No. 3 has been banned for some uses because it caused tumors in rats. Other dyes are also under investigation.

It's good to know that no single food additive poses a severe danger to the entire population. But several additives, such as those we have mentioned, do pose some risks to the general public and should be avoided as much as possible. Fortunately, people are more aware than ever of the dangers of pesticide residues on fruits and vegetables and of additives in our processed foods. There is intense pressure on the federal government to ban unsafe substances. But it is also our responsibility as consumers to read labels and be aware of what we're putting into our bodies, and to learn how to eat safe and healthy food for long and healthy lives.

Vocabulary

Select the letter of the answer that is closest in meaning to the italicized word or phrase.

1. We like to have pepperoni without *mold.*
   a. yellow fat
   b. strange spices
   c. greenish growth
   d. reddish color

2. The *controversy* surrounding additives is nothing new.
   a. purpose
   b. debate
   c. idea
   d. judgment

3. *Fake* China tea was often made from dried thorn leaves colored with a poisonous substance.
   a. Imitation
   b. Cheap
   c. Ordinary
   d. Light

4. Even candy was *contaminated* with highly poisonous salts.
   a. injured
   b. destroyed
   c. diseased
   d. made impure

5. What happens when we consume this *conglomeration* of chemicals?
   a. arrangement
   b. collection
   c. discovery
   d. preference

6. The average American *ingests* about five pounds of additives per year.
   a. cleans in the body
   b. changes to liquid
   c. takes in as food
   d. discharges from the body

7. Studies have shown that some babies cannot *metabolize* one of the substances that aspartame is made from.
   a. change into energy
   b. grow with
   c. sleep with
   d. live on

8. All the colored breakfast cereals for kids are *loaded with* food dyes.
   a. made out of
   b. destroyed by
   c. improved with
   d. packed with

9. No single food additive *poses* a severe danger to the entire population.
   a. transmits
   b. maintains
   c. presents
   d. donates

10. People are aware of the dangers of pesticide *residues* on fruits and vegetables.
    a. remainders
    b. samples
    c. trash
    d. portions

Vocabulary Extension

Part A

Read the list of nouns below. Match one item from each column to make sentences similar to those used in the reading.

Noun	*Verb Phrase*	*Object*
1. chemicals	a. has been linked to	g. mustard husks
2. pepper	b. was mixed with	h. cancer
3. tea	c. are added to	i. copper salts
4. candy	d. was contaminated with	j. food dyes
5. saccharin	e. are loaded with	k. everything we eat
6. breakfast cereals	f. was adulterated with	l. dried leaves

1. chemicals   _c_   _k_   Chemicals are added to everything we eat.

2. pepper   ___   ___   _____

3. tea   ___   ___   _____

4. candy   ___   ___   _____

5. saccharin   ___   ___   _____

6. breakfast cereals   ___   ___   _____

Part B

Now make a question out of each of the sentences in Part A.

Example:

What is added to everything we eat?

With a partner, take turns asking and answering these questions.

Part C

Use the verb phrases from Part A to make your own sentences about food additives.

Comprehension

Looking for the Main Ideas

Circle the letter of the best answer.

1. What is the main idea of paragraph 2?
   a. Food additives are chemical substances.
   b. Some suppliers adulterate food to save money.
   c. Food adulteration has a long and sometimes dangerous history.
   d. Even something as innocent-looking as candy can be dangerous if it has additives.

2. Paragraph 7 is mostly about
   a. how phenylalanine can cause brain problems and behavior changes.
   b. the fact that lawsuits have failed to block the use of aspartame.
   c. the uses of the sugar substitute aspartame.
   d. the dangers posed by the substances in some artificial sweeteners.

3. Paragraph 9 is mainly concerned with
   a. the questionable safety of food dyes.
   b. the money-saving value of artificial flavorings and colorings.
   c. the banning of toxic and cancer-causing food dyes.
   d. the most popular foods in which dyes are used.

Skimming and Scanning for Details

Scan the reading to find the answers to these questions. Write complete answers.

1. What are five reasons why additives are put into food?

2. According to the reading, why was tea adulterated in 18th-century London?

3. What negative effect does gassing have on tomatoes?

4. What are five categories of food additives and their uses?

5. In the last sentence of paragraph 6, what does the word *these* refer to?

6. What is a common use of NutraSweet?

7. To what does the word *its* in paragraph 8, sentence 2, refer?

8. Why does the use of nitrite in bacon pose a special problem?

9. Give two reasons why dyes are widely used in foods.

10. Why has Red No. 3 been banned for some uses?

Making Inferences and Drawing Conclusions

The answers to these questions are not directly stated in the reading. Circle the letter of the best answer.

1. The reading implies that
    a. today's food additives are more dangerous than those used in the past.
    b. economics has always played a role in the use of food additives.
    c. food additives have more to do with making food look good than anything else.
    d. regulations on food purity have eliminated most problems with food adulteration.

2. From the reading, it can be concluded that
    a. the health risks posed by some additives must be weighed against their positive values, such as food preservation.
    b. Americans gain weight as a result of the large amount of food additives they consume.
    c. the majority of food additives are bad for us and should be banned.
    d. there is no evidence to prove that banning certain additives reduces the risk of cancer.

3. It can be inferred from the reading that
    a. when questions of safety are involved, getting a substance banned is a quick and easy process.
    b. there is no reason to be concerned about the safety of food additives because the government is doing all it can to protect consumers against unsafe substances.
    c. the goal of some consumer groups is to pressure the government to ban all forms of food adulteration.
    d. in spite of the government's role in regulating food additives, our health and safety also depend on our own education and awareness.

4. The author's purpose is to
    a. entertain.   c. persuade.
    b. inform.   d. argue.

Discussion

Discuss these questions with your classmates.
1. Are there some foods that you think are safer than others?
2. What are some of your favorite foods? Say why you like them.
3. Have you ever been sick as a result of eating or drinking a particular type of food? Describe what it did to you and the possible causes.
4. If you had a choice between food that didn't look very appetizing and was more expensive but was healthy and food that looked good and appetizing but was chemically treated, which would you choose and why?

BST and Milk Yield

The following article by Nigel Collins was published in the journal Catalyst: GCSE Science Review *(volume 12, issue 3, February 1, 2002). This journal is published by Philip Allan Updates as an educational resource providing articles on key science topics for the General Certificate of School Education in the United Kingdom.*

Pesticides and growth-promoting chemicals are used to improve crop yields. Farm animals may also be treated with chemicals to improve yield. There are both advantages to and justified concerns about the use of such substances. You will study these in your GCSE science course. In this 'For debate' we look at the science involved and the issues raised by the use of a hormone to improve milk yield in cattle.

Somatotropins are hormones involved in the growth and development of mammals. Bovine somatotropin (BST) is a growth hormone produced by cows. It is secreted into a cow's blood from the pituitary gland at the base of the brain. Cows with a naturally high milk yield often have high BST levels. In the 1930s it was found that injecting a lactating cow (one producing milk) with BST increased its yield. BST is injected because it is a protein, like insulin.[1] If proteins are given by mouth they are broken down by digestion in the gut.

> **Hormones** are substances made by endocrine glands. They are released into the bloodstream in minute amounts. The blood circulates them to target organs where their effects are slow, widespread and often long-lasting.

---

[1]insulin = a hormone that regulates glucose in the blood.

Injecting BST looks like a useful way of increasing the milk yield from herds of dairy cows. BST is made by biotechnology using genetic engineering or recombinant DNA technology. The gene encoding BST is inserted into a bacterium, a strain of E. coli. The bacteria grow rapidly in a fermenter[2] and, because they carry the BST gene, they make lots of BST.

HOW DOES BST WORK?

One effect of BST is to cause the liver to secrete another substance, insulin-like growth factor (IGF). Human and bovine ST differ in structure, but IGF is the same in both cow and human. It is not clear how IGF causes increased milk production but increased blood flow to the mammary glands, and increase in the number of mammary cells or an increase in mammary cell activity could be involved. Cows need to eat more if they are making more milk and it has been shown that they consume 10–20% more food—grass, hay or corn.

A cow will produce milk for about 300 days after calving,[3] providing it is milked regularly after the calf[4] is taken away. Peak production is reached at about 7–9 weeks. BST maintains milk yields at higher levels for longer and so could improve yield by around 10% or more.

WHERE IS BST USED?

BST was approved for use in the USA in 1994 and in many countries round the world since. Cows that give a lower milk yield are injected every 14–28 days after their natural lactation[5] has peaked. Canada and the European Union (EU), including the UK, do not allow the use of BST. The EU stated that if BST was allowed it should be by prescription, with veterinary advice on which animals could be treated. Why doesn't the EU allow BST while other countries do?

CONCERNS

There are four areas of concern.

---

[2]fermenter = scientific equipment designed to exclude oxygen and encourage the growth of bacteria.

[3]calving = giving birth to a baby cow.

[4]calf = young cow.

[5]lactation = production of milk by cows.

Human Health

Could BST or IGF pass into milk from cows, and could they be harmful to people drinking the milk? Both hormones are proteins and should be digested, not absorbed, so there should not be a problem.

Cattle treated with BST have a slightly higher chance of mastitis which is a painful bacterial disease of the udder.[6] BST does not cause mastitis directly but the disease is more likely in high-yielding cows. The treatment for mastitis includes using antibiotics. Increased antibiotic use is undesirable because it might increase the incidence of antibiotic-resistant strains of bacteria, and reduce the usefulness of antibiotics in treating human disease.

In the UK it was felt that, because BST increases IGF levels to above normal and IGF is a hormone active in humans whose effects are widespread and difficult to measure, BST should continue to be banned. Many people feel that we should not introduce things until we are certain there will be no untoward effects.

IGF levels in milk from BST-treated cows rise by between 25 and 70%. This sounds dramatic, but in fact we produce IGF all the time and the levels in our own saliva[7] are greater than that in milk. However there are concerns about possible increased risks of some forms of cancer when IGF levels are higher.

An expert panel in Canada in 1999 felt there was 'no significant risk to human safety from eating products from BST treated animals.'

Animal Health and Welfare

Another expert panel in Canada felt that BST presented 'a sufficient and unacceptable threat to the safety of dairy cows.' This was based on the increased incidence of mastitis. There also appear to be increased foot problems in treated cattle. On these grounds BST use was still not allowed. Europe takes a similar position, though this runs counter to an assessment made by the European Commission's Committee for Veterinary Medicinal Products.

Labelling

Many people think that milk from BST-treated cows should be labelled. In the USA it has been argued that milk in cartons is from many different sources, some using BST and some not, so labelling would be

---

[6]udder = part of cow where milk is stored.

[7]saliva = liquid in the mouth which helps us to swallow food.

too difficult and is not justified. This same argument has been used about labelling genetically modified maize or soy products, but such foods are appropriately labelled and customers can make their choice. Small-scale farmers producing cartons of milk from untreated cows are allowed to label them, but only if the information is 'truthful and not misleading.'

Socioeconomic Aspects

The debate centres[8] on the effects of BST on farm organisation and whether farmers with small herds would be better or worse off if BST were used. BST is not authorised in Europe at the time of writing. If the USA were to ship dairy products to Britain on a large scale it is likely that commercial pressure would be applied to allow the import of milk from treated cows. This in turn would put pressure on European farmers.

In the meantime—what do you think? Should cows in Britain and the rest of Europe be injected with BST to increase milk production?

---

[8]Note the small differences in spelling and punctuation between the British English used in this article and American English.

Vocabulary

Look at the reading to answer the following questions.

1. Which word is closest in meaning to *yield* in paragraph 1?
   a. manufacture
   c. production
   b. income
   d. arrival

2. In paragraph 1, what does *concerns* mean?
   a. fears
   c. ideas
   b. matters
   d. restrictions

3. Which word in paragraph 2 means "intestines"?

4. Which word in paragraph 3 means "groups of cows"?

5. Which of these words is similar in meaning to *inserted* as used in paragraph 3?
   a. started
   c. contained
   b. introduced
   d. included

6. What does the word *peak* in paragraph 5 mean?
   a. better
   b. top
   c. helpful
   d. nice

7. Which word in paragraph 6 refers to a doctor who takes care of animals?

8. Which of these words is closest in meaning to *incidence* as used in paragraph 9?
   a. total
   b. frequency
   c. cause
   d. power

9. Which of these words is similar in meaning to *counter* as used in paragraph 13?
   a. parallel
   b. similar
   c. unequal
   d. opposite

10. Which word in paragraph 13 means "evaluation"?

Vocabulary Extension

Part A

The reading contains several compound adjectives. Match the pairs below. Then look back at the reading to check your answers.

1. long-_____
2. insulin-_____
3. high-_____
4. antibiotic-_____
5. small-_____

a. like
b. lasting
c. scale
d. yielding
e. resistant

Part B

Use one half of each compound above with a different word to complete each sentence below.

1. A crop that is resistant to insects is _____.

2. Something that is like a human is _____.

3. Farms that have large quantities of land and crops are _____.

4. A tradition or custom that has stood for a long time is _____.

5. An official with a high rank is _____.

Comprehension

Looking for the Main Ideas

Circle the letter of the answer that best completes the sentence.

1. BST _____.
   a. improves the quality of milk
   b. increases milk production
   c. is a hormone that is not produced by cows
   d. helps cows digest

2. BST is used _____.
   a. in Canada and the United States
   b. in the United States and some other countries
   c. in Europe
   d. in Canada and Europe

3. A panel in Canada thinks that BST _____.
   a. is not safe for cows
   b. makes cows healthier
   c. gives people mastitis
   d. has no effects on cattle or people

4. Milk from BST-treated cows is _____.
   a. difficult to label
   b. always labeled
   c. impossible to label
   d. labeled only in the United States

Skimming and Scanning for Details

Scan the reading quickly to find the answers to these questions. Write complete answers.

1. What is one effect of BST?

2. How long does a cow produce milk after calving?

3. When does a cow produce the most milk naturally?

4. When did they find that injecting cows with BST increased milk production?

5. How often are cows injected with BST after their natural lactation?

6. By how much could BST improve milk yields?

7. When was BST approved for use in the United States?

8. What is used to treat mastitis in cows?

9. Why does the United States think it is too difficult to label milk cartons?

10. Who is allowed to label cartons of milk from untreated cows?

Making Inferences and Drawing Conclusions

Some of the following statements can be inferred from the reading, and others cannot. Circle the number of each statement that can be inferred.

1. There isn't enough evidence against BST to stop its use completely.

2. Milk from the United States is more likely to have BST than milk from Europe.

3. Europeans are more concerned about food safety than Americans.

4. Cows treated with BST are more likely to have mastitis than those not treated with BST.

5. The use of BST can indirectly affect the health of humans.

6. The question of the safety of BST has caused worldwide debate.

7. Giving cows antibiotics will make humans safer from disease.

8. Europeans are more concerned about animal welfare and safety than Americans.

9. It is not in the interest of large-scale U.S. dairy farms to label food containing BST.

10. People in the United Kingdom believe that until the effects of BST are known for sure, it should be banned.

Discussion

Discuss these questions with your classmates.
1. Do you know of any other animals that are harmed by methods used to make them more productive?
2. What do you think the government should do to control the safety of our food supply?
3. Why do you think that substances like BST and pesticides are allowed to be used?

Writing a Summary

Write a one-paragraph summary of Reading 1. Check your summary with the Summary Checklist on page 273.

Paraphrasing

Paraphrase the last paragraph (The debate . . .) in Reading 2. Look at pages 267–270 to find out about paraphrasing. Begin paraphrasing with either "According to the *Catalyst,* . . ." or "Based on an article in the *Catalyst,* . . . ."

Research

Choose a particular food or drink additive and find out three effects it has, or choose a disease and find three things that cause it.
The following are suggested topics:

Effects of lead poisoning	Effects of caffeine
Effects of vitamin supplements	Effects of DDT use
Causes of obesity	Causes of anorexia

You may use your research later to write a cause-and-effect essay.

Student Essay

Read the following essay written by a student.

The Negative Sides of Fast Food

With today's fast lifestyle, it is very hard to keep up with the traditional way of taking care of all human needs. Eating habits are no exception. According to an article in *Success* magazine (November 1994), America today eats more fast food than ever before. Ninety-six out of every one hundred Americans eat fast food on some kind of regular basis. There are many side effects related to this popular eating habit, most of which are damaging to our health and personal care. Eating fast food regularly may cause our bodies to be deficient in the vitamins and minerals we need to maintain good health; also, eating fast food can be very addictive, and people accustomed to it rarely change their eating habits.

The food sold in most fast food restaurants may not be all that good for us. The majority of those restaurants are franchises, which means that everything has to look, taste, and smell the same way in all the restaurants of a particular franchise. A franchise controls this by having a main food distribution center, which implies that the food has to go through a long frozen storage period, then a transportation period before it gets to the consumer. In order for the food to still taste fresh after all this time, a lot of artificial preservatives have to be added. As if that were not enough, the main element that the fast food market advertises and competes for is not good food or fresh ingredients, but lowest prices, and we all know what that means.

People who have the habit of eating fast food rarely even try to change their diet. Instead, people tend to get more and more used to the convenience and taste of fast food. According to a survey in *Industrial and Labor Relations Review* magazine (October 1992), out of every ten fast food eaters, only four will eat the same amount or less, and the other six will double their "loads" of fast food within four years; and out of every ten people who finally get to control their eating disorder, six will come back to eating fast food within six years. These alarming figures seem to be in contradiction with today's convenient ways of cooking at home. Easy-to-make dishes like those for microwaves, soups, etc., would appear to be the solution for the fast food problem, but obviously the real problem is not the trouble of cooking at home, but the addicting simplicity of fast food.

In conclusion, eating fast food is not only an unhealthy habit but also a corrupting one. Chances are most of us will have to eat some kind of fast food over a period in our lives, but this would not be a problem if we planned a diet that could be combined with fast food. Simple meals such as cereals, yogurts, and dishes for microwave ovens can make a big difference and are just as fast and affordable as food from any of the popular franchises. All it takes is a little conscience and responsibility.

Pedro
Dominican Republic

Student Essay Follow-Up

1. Underline the thesis statement.
2. What two effects of eating fast food is the writer considering?
3. What is the topic sentence of paragraph 2? Is it clearly supported?
4. What effect is the writer considering in paragraph 3? What evidence of the effect does he give?
5. In the conclusion, does the writer restate the thesis statement in other words?

Organizing: The Cause-and-Effect Essay

Another popular type of essay is the cause-and-effect essay. This form is frequently used in academic writing. In college, your history teacher may ask you to write about the causes of the American Civil War; your biology teacher may ask you to write on the three effects of a snake bite; your psychology teacher may ask you to explain the high rate of alcoholism among American Indians.

There are three types of cause-and-effect essays:

1. the cause analysis essay explains causes.
2. the effect analysis essay explains effects.
3. the causal chain essay explains causes that lead to effects in a chain.

The Cause Analysis Essay

There are few situations that can be traced back to a single cause. Something usually has several causes or a combination of causes that lead to an effect.

For example, consider this question: Why do some children have a low IQ? For some, it may be a result of early malnutrition, which slows brain growth; for others, it may be a result of exposure to toxins, such as lead, which damage the nervous system. It may be caused by the lack of a stimulating environment. It may also be caused by parents who do not encourage their children or spend time with them. If you examined the topic further, you might find that family size could also be a cause.

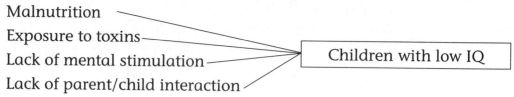

Malnutrition
Exposure to toxins
Lack of mental stimulation
Lack of parent/child interaction

Children with low IQ

The Thesis Statement
The thesis statement should state the causes to be discussed.

Example:

Low IQ in children is generally caused by the following factors: malnutrition in childhood, lack of a stimulating environment, and lack of interaction with their parents.

Then you might go on to comment on the causes.

Although there are other causes for low IQ in children, these were picked out as the more important causes and the ones that could be easily supported.

The Body Paragraphs
Each body paragraph should discuss one of the causes mentioned in the thesis statement.

The Conclusion
The conclusion should restate the thesis and provide a general comment on the topic.

The Effect Analysis Essay

Just as there can be many causes for something, a cause can have several effects. For example, many people consume caffeine in one form or another, which has the effect of making them alert, but addiction to caffeine can have many negative effects such as restlessness, insomnia, heartbeat irregularities, and even high blood pressure, which may lead to other serious problems.

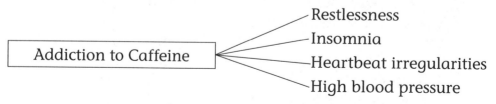

Addiction to Caffeine

Restlessness
Insomnia
Heartbeat irregularities
High blood pressure

In the student essay "The Negative Sides of Fast Food," you can see the two negative effects of eating fast food regularly. In Reading 1, the effects of food additives are explained. Notice that reference is made to the cause before explaining the effect. It is important to understand which is the cause and which is the effect. Look at the following examples:

Cause: The additives sodium nitrite and sodium nitrate are two closely related chemicals that have been used for centuries to preserve meat.

Effect: Nitrite has been considered an important cause of stomach cancer in the United States, Japan, and other countries.

Cause: The sugar substitute aspartame is sold commercially as Equal or NutraSweet and is used in many diet beverages.

Effect: About one out of 20,000 babies cannot metabolize one of the two substances that aspartame is made from, and toxic levels of that substance can result in mental retardation.

Effect: Some people who have consumed aspartame have reported dizziness, headaches, and even seizures.

Effect: Aspartame may be linked to an increased risk of brain tumors.

Exercise 1

Identify which is the cause (C) and which is the effect (E).

1. _____ Accident death rates dropped by 30 percent.

   _____ A seat belt law was passed.

   _____ Motorists were required to wear seat belts.

2. _____ Carla burned 500 calories per week.

   _____ Carla's blood pressure was lower.

   _____ Carla exercised 45 minutes each day.

3. ___ Social and work-related pressures have increased in modern times.

   ___ People are more at risk for stress-related illnesses, such as heart attacks.

4. ___ The sun's ultraviolet rays penetrate the deeper layer of the skin.

   ___ Skin cancer is one of the most common forms of cancer in the United States.

   ___ The protective ozone layer in the atmosphere is decreased by pollutants.

5. ___ Most American women over the age of 50 consume half of their daily calcium requirements.

   ___ Calcium in bones is gradually depleted, leaving them weak and brittle, a condition called osteoporosis.

   ___ In this country, older women suffer approximately five million fractures each year.

6. ___ People who walk daily have healthier cardiovascular systems.

   ___ Aerobic exercises allow the heart and lungs to utilize oxygen more efficiently.

7. ___ Flu viruses are highly contagious and are spread through close contact with infected persons.

   ___ Flu epidemics spread rapidly through the workplace.

8. ___ Antibiotics have been overprescribed by doctors for decades.

   ___ Over a period of time, bacteria can become resistant to antibiotics when repeatedly exposed to them.

   ___ A medical crisis exists because many antibiotics are no longer useful for combatting diseases.

In each sentence of the paragraph, underline the cause once and the effect twice.

1. Ear pain occurs when there is a buildup of fluid and pressure in the middle ear. Often during a cold or an allergy attack, particularly in small children, the ear tube becomes swollen shut, preventing the normal flow of fluid from the middle ear. Fluid begins to accumulate, causing stuffiness and decreased hearing. Sometimes a bacterial infection starts in the fluid, resulting in pain and fever. Ear pain and ear stuffiness can also result from high altitudes, such as when flying in an airplane or driving in the mountains. Swallowing will frequently relieve the pressure in the ear tube.

2. Eating candy can produce acids in the body. Consuming carbohydrates can even produce an alcoholic condition in your body. One of our great orators, William Jennings Bryan, gave speeches nationwide about the bad effects of drinking alcohol, causing more than one person to change his drinking habits. Ironically, Bryan himself died of an alcoholic stomach as a result of eating 13 pancakes with syrup for breakfast. Eating the pancakes, which are full of carbohydrates, and the sugary syrup created a kind of alcoholic brew in his stomach. This innocently consumed brew produced alcohol poisoning, which in turn led to his death.

3. Exercise is the central ingredient of good health because it tones the muscles, strengthens the bones, makes the heart and lungs work better, and prevents disease. It increases energy and vitality and gives you a good feeling about yourself. This sense of well-being helps you deal better with stress, eases depression, and aids sleep. There are three kinds of exercises, of which *strengthening* is the least important because it builds more bulky muscles, although it increases general strength. *Stretching* exercises keep the muscles loose and are a bit more important than weight-lifting. Stretching

before doing other kinds of exercises warms up the muscles and makes them looser and less susceptible to injury. *Aerobic* exercises are the key to fitness because they improve your heart and lungs. Your heart speeds up to pump larger amounts of blood. You breathe more frequently and more deeply to increase the oxygen transfer from the lungs to the blood. As a result of these efforts, the heart becomes larger and stronger and your lungs healthier.

The Thesis Statement

As in the causal analysis essay, the thesis statement of an effect analysis essay should state the effects to be discussed.

Example:

Eating fast food regularly may cause our bodies to be deficient in vitamins and minerals we need to maintain good health; also, eating fast food can be very addictive, and people accustomed to it rarely change their eating habits.

The Body Paragraphs

As for a cause analysis essay, select two or three major effects. In the thesis statement above, two effects have been selected. Therefore, the first body paragraph will explain the effects on health of eating fast food, and the second body paragraph will explain the addictive effect of eating fast food regularly. Support each effect with relevant examples and/or facts.

The Conclusion

The conclusion should restate the thesis and provide a general comment on the topic.

The Causal Chain Essay

In the causal chain type of cause-and-effect essay, one cause leads to an effect, which leads to another cause, and so on, creating a chain of causes and effects.

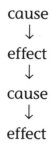

cause
↓
effect
↓
cause
↓
effect

For example, bad weather conditions such as excessive rainfall may affect farmers' vegetable crops, causing the vegetable crops to die. This makes vegetables scarce, causing prices to rise in the supermarkets. This results in people's not buying very many vegetables because they are so expensive. Since people eat fewer vegetables, their health is affected.

excessive rainfall
↓
damage to vegetable crops
↓
vegetable prices go up
↓
people eat less vegetables
↓
people are not as healthy

In Reading 2, a causal chain may be implied: Cows are given BST to increase their production of milk. The BST causes the cows to get infections, so the cows are given antibiotics. The antibiotics in turn get into our milk supply, creating cause for alarm.

cows are given BST to increase milk production
↓
cows get infections
↓
cows are given antibiotics
↓
antibiotics get into our milk supply

The most frequent use of this type of essay is in the sciences—for example, in essays about biological or weather cycles.

Plan the causal chain for one of the topics below or for another topic from geography or biology.

1. The cutting of forests in the Amazon
2. The killing of elephants for ivory

The Thesis Statement
The thesis statement should state the three or four steps in the chain:

Example:

The use of BST to increase milk production indirectly affects human health, since the cows that are given BST get infections and are treated with antibiotics, which then get into our milk supply.

The Body Paragraphs

It is important to break the chain into three or four major steps. Each body paragraph should describe one step in the chain stated in the thesis statement. Each step should be supported with details.

The Conclusion

The conclusion should restate the main points in the chain and provide a comment on the topic.

Writing Practice

Choose one of the following topics.

1. Write a cause-and-effect essay on one of the topics you researched in this chapter.
2. Write an effect analysis essay on eating junk food regularly, focusing on three effects.
3. Write an essay on the causes or effects of pollution.
4. Write an essay on the causes or effects of the use of pesticides.

1. Pre-writing.

   Work alone, with a partner, or in a group.

   a. Brainstorm the topic. Choose a pre-writing technique you prefer.
   b. Brainstorm for three causes or three effects.
   c. Work on a thesis statement.

2. Develop an outline.

   a. Organize your ideas.

      Step 1: Write your thesis statement. Include the three causes or effects.

      Step 2: Order the causes or effects.

      Step 3: Provide supporting ideas and details for each cause or effect.

   b. Make a more detailed outline. The essay outline on page 22 will help you.

3. Write a rough draft.

   Look at page 261 to find out about writing a rough draft.

4. Revise your rough draft.

   Use the checklist on page 262.

5. Edit your essay.

> Check your work for fragments (sentences that are not complete).

> **Example:**
>> *Error:* Although I try to eat fresh food.
>>
>> *Correct:* Although I try to eat fresh food, it is easier to buy pre-packaged food.

> When you find a mistake of this type, you can use the symbol "frag" (fragment). Look at page 263 for other symbols to use when editing your work.

6. Write your final copy.

Video Activity • Organic Food Labels

1. The video discusses the types of labels used to indicate that food is organic, not contaminated with pesticides and other harmful chemicals. Do you believe that organic food is much safer than other types of food?

2. Review these words used in the video: *ban* (verb), *irradiate* (verb), *synthetic* (adjective).

3. After you watch the video, discuss these questions.

   a. What does the term *organic* mean? List at least three processes or ingredients whose use is prohibited in organic foods. What dangers do these processes or ingredients pose?

   b. Does a food product have to be 100% organic in order to be labeled "organic"?

   c. Are foods that are certified as organic necessarily better?

   d. How much more expensive are organic foods than those not certified as organic?

   e. How does the new labeling law benefit shoppers?

4. The new law described in the video will make it easier for consumers to identify healthy, organic foods and understand exactly what the label "organic" means. Discuss the effects of the new labels on one or both of the following: people's health and the price of groceries. Explain these effects in a journal entry or short report.

Internet Activity

- Use the Internet to find two different web sites that offer information on "organic food." Who created the web sites and what information do they provide?

- How are the two web sites different in content and presentation? Which web site did you think was more reliable and why?

CHAPTER 8

Issues for Debate

Pre-Reading Questions

Discuss these questions.

1. How do animals help humans?
2. Are all animals the same, or are some more important than others?
3. Do you agree with society's treatment of animals?

1. Which of the animals shown above do you think is the most intelligent, and why?
2. Which animal is the most useful to humans?
3. Which animal is the friendliest?
4. Describe some other ways in which humans use animals.

Animal Rights

The American Declaration of Independence said that "all men are created equal, that they are endowed . . . with certain inalienable rights, that among these are Life, Liberty and the pursuit of Happiness." This was one of the first statements of human rights. Back in 1776, this was a new idea, but today we are used to the idea that as humans we have certain basic rights.

Our right to equal treatment also means that we have to treat other people as equals. In the beginning, equal rights and responsibilities were limited to certain groups. Over time, justice prevailed, and with the civil rights movement came the modern belief that it is not acceptable to discriminate on the grounds of sex, race, or religion.

Does the belief in equality, freedom, and the right to be treated in a certain way apply to animals as well? Do animals also have "certain inalienable rights" among which are "Life, Liberty and the pursuit of Happiness"? This issue is at the heart of the debate about animal rights.

Animal welfare societies started in Britain and the United States in the early 1800s. In fact, the United Kingdom passed laws to protect animals from abuse before there were any laws to protect children. The Royal Society for the Prevention of Cruelty to Animals (RSPCA) was founded in 1824 to find and punish people who deliberately harmed animals. The first book on animal rights was written by an Englishman, Henry Salt, in 1892. His book and the animal rights movement that he started were based on two ideas: that human beings are not made to eat meat and that we have a moral duty to treat animals "like us." This means we should behave toward animals just as we behave toward other human beings. Not everybody supported Salt's ideas, but he made people think about animals and their rights.

In 1948, human rights became universal with the United Nations Declaration of Human Rights, which stated that "recognition of the inherent dignity and of the equal and inalienable rights of all members of the human family is the foundation of freedom, justice and peace in the world." But it is only since the 1970s that the idea of animals having rights just as humans do has developed. It started with an essay written by Peter Singer in which he used the term "animal liberation." In his article in the *New York Review of Books,* Singer wrote about how animals should be treated, and this started the debate that continues up to now.

How similar are animals to humans? Can some animals feel and think in ways similar to humans? Scientists have discovered that chimpanzees have many similarities with humans. Researchers who work with chimpanzees say they experience almost every emotion we do. They use tools, think ahead, and take care of one another. At Central Washington University in the United States, a chimpanzee named Washoe has learned American Sign Language; he uses it to communicate with humans and has even taught it to another chimpanzee called Loulis. Researchers also claim that other creatures, such as gorillas, whales, and dolphins, are more like us than we think. On May 20, 2003, the BBC reported on a study published in the U.S. journal *Proceedings of the National Academy of Sciences,* which claims chimpanzees are so closely related to humans that they should properly be considered members of the human family. Scientists from Wayne State University's School of Medicine in Detroit, Michigan, examined key genes in humans and several ape species and found them to be 99.4 percent the same as those of chimpanzees.

A British animal welfare group called Compassion in World Farming (CIWF) started campaigning in the 1980s to win a new status in law for animals. They wanted animals to be given the status of "sentient beings" (i.e., possessing a level of conscious awareness and able to have feelings). After years of petitions, the concept that animals are sentient was finally recognized by the European Union in 1997. A statement was added to the treaty that established the EU, recognizing animals as sentient beings and requiring that their welfare be properly taken into account in the development of the Community's policies on agriculture, transport, the internal market, and research. Compassion in World Farming accepts that farm animals will be killed for their meat but argues that they should be treated humanely. As reported by the BBC on May 9, 2003, the group believes that animals that live in communities "often exhibit signs of morality that resemble human behavior. There is evidence that some animals do have some level of morality and some concern over other animals. Living within a group requires a moral code of behavior. Zoologists who have spent their professional lives studying animal behavior, either by observation or by experiments to test their mental capacities, believe that many animals feel and think." Joyce D'Silva, chief executive of CIWF, told BBC *News Online,* "This has huge implications for the ways we use animals and implies that all farm animals are entitled to humane lives and deaths."

If it is true that some creatures have a capacity for consciousness similar to that of human beings, then there is justification for giving them rights like those of humans.

Germany has become the first European nation to vote to guarantee animal rights in its constitution. Before the vote, animals in Germany were already protected by laws governing the conditions under which they could be held in captivity. The issue of animal rights had been debated among German politicians for years. Then, in 2002, lawmakers in Germany voted to add "and animals" to a clause that obliges the state to respect and protect the dignity of humans. With this new law, there will be tighter restrictions on the use of animals for testing cosmetics and nonprescription drugs. Lawmakers in Germany said that they would give more funding to projects that look at alternatives to using animals for experiments.

Today, animal welfare groups around the world continue with their work to change laws to protect animals and make their existence more humane.

Vocabulary

Select the letter of the answer that is closest in meaning to the italicized word or phrase.

1. All men are *endowed with* certain inalienable rights.
    a. gifted with
    b. intelligent enough to have
    c. capable of
    d. lacking in

2. All men have the right to "Life, Liberty, and the *pursuit of Happiness.*"
    a. search for
    b. judgment of
    c. answer to
    d. decision for

3. Over time, justice *prevailed.*
    a. failed
    b. succeeded
    c. existed
    d. lived

4. This *issue* is at the heart of the debate about animal rights.
    a. question
    b. doubt
    c. danger
    d. answer

5. The United Kingdom passed laws to protect animals from *abuse*.
   a. anger
   b. attack
   c. mistreatment
   d. worry

6. The RSPCA was founded to punish people who *deliberately* harmed animals.
   a. intentionally
   b. forcefully
   c. accidentally
   d. strongly

7. Chimpanzees have a richly developed *consciousness*.
   a. knowledge
   b. awareness
   c. memory
   d. order

8. Compassion in World Farming started campaigning to win a new *status* in law for animals.
   a. purpose
   b. degree
   c. position
   d. level

9. CIWF argues that animals should be treated *humanely*.
   a. politely
   b. cruelly
   c. generously
   d. caringly

10. With this new law, there will be tighter *restrictions on* the use of animals for testing.
    a. limitations on
    b. methods for
    c. areas for
    d. systems for

Vocabulary Extension

Part A

Find at least one adjective that was used in the reading before each noun below. Add some more of your own.

1. RIGHTS

   human____rights   _____ rights
   _____ rights   _____ rights

2. TREATMENT

_____ treatment   _____ treatment

_____ treatment   _____ treatment

3. DUTY

_____ duty   _____ duty

_____ duty   _____ duty

4. CODE

_____ code   _____ code

_____ code   _____ code

5. NEEDS

_____ needs   _____ needs

_____ needs   _____ needs

Part B

Using the phrases above, take turns asking and answering questions about the reading.

Comprehension

Looking for the Main Ideas

Write complete answers to the following questions.

1. Which paragraph describes the main issue affecting the debate about animal rights?

2. What was Henry Salt's philosophy?

3. How have developments in human rights influenced ideas and opinions about animal rights?

4. What aspects of our treatment of animals are called into question by animal rights groups?

Skimming and Scanning for Details

Scan the reading to find the answers to these questions. Write complete answers.

1. What were the aims of the RSPCA?

2. How did the issue of animal rights start to become discussed?

3. In what ways have researchers tried to compare animals and humans?

4. In what ways has Germany done more than other countries to protect animals?

Making Inferences and Drawing Conclusions

The answers to these questions are not directly stated in the article. Write complete answers.

1. What conclusion do you draw from the fact that, in Britain, laws protecting animals preceded laws protecting children?

2. How are prevention of suffering to animals and meat-eating related?

3. How might gorillas, whales, and dolphins be like humans?

Discussion

Discuss these questions with your classmates.
1. Do humans have to eat meat?
2. How similar are animals to humans, in your opinion?
3. Should animals be used for medical research?
4. Do you think animals' rights should be protected by law?
5. Do you think the term "moral behavior" can be used to describe the behavior of animals? Why or why not?

Clone Farm

The following article by Andrea Graves appeared in the New Scientist, *August 18, 2001.*

Billions of identical chickens could soon be rolling off production lines. Factory farming could soon enter a new era of mass production. Companies in the US are developing the technology needed to "clone" chickens on a massive scale.

Once a chicken with desirable traits has been bred or genetically engineered, tens of thousands of eggs, which will hatch into identical copies, could roll off the production lines every hour. Billions of clones could be produced each year to supply chicken farms with birds that all grow at the same rate, have the same amount of meat and taste the same.

This, at least, is the vision of the US's National Institute of Science and Technology, which has given Origen Therapeutics of Burlingame, California, and Embrex of North Carolina $4.7 million to help fund research. The prospect has alarmed animal welfare groups, who fear it could increase the suffering of farm birds.

That's unlikely to put off the poultry industry, however, which wants disease-resistant birds that grow faster on less food. "Producers would like the same meat quantity but to use reduced inputs to get there," says Mike Fitzgerald of Origen.

To meet this demand, Origen aims to "create an animal that is effectively a clone", he says. Normal cloning doesn't work in birds because eggs can't be removed and implanted. Instead, the company is trying to bulk-grow embryonic stem cells taken from fertilised eggs as soon as they're laid. "The trick is to culture the cells without them starting to differentiate, so they remain pluripotent,[1]" says Fitzgerald.

Using a long-established technique, these donor[2] cells will then be injected into the embryo of a freshly laid, fertilised recipient egg, forming a chick that is a "chimera." Strictly speaking a chimera isn't a clone, because it contains cells from both donor and recipient. But Fitzgerald says it will be enough if, say, 95 per cent of a chicken's body develops from donor cells. "In the poultry world, it doesn't matter if it's not 100 per cent," he says.

With its patent still at application stage, Origen is unwilling to reveal if it can reliably obtain such chimeras. But it has occasionally created the ideal: chicks that are 100 per cent donor-derived, or pure clones.

Another challenge for Origen is to scale up production. To do this, it has teamed up with Embrex, which produces machines that can inject vaccines into up to 50,000 eggs an hour. Embrex is now trying to modify the machines to locate the embryo and inject the cells into precisely the right spot without killing it. Automating the process will be tricky, admits Nandini Mandu of Embrex. Even when it's done by hand, up to 75 per cent of the embryos die.

In [the] future, Origen envisages freezing stem cells from different strains[3] of chicken. If orders come in for a particular strain, millions of eggs could be produced in months or even weeks. At present, maintaining all the varieties the market might call for is too expensive for breeders, and it takes years to breed enough chickens to produce the billions of eggs that farmers need.

Fitzgerald insists that genetic modification isn't on Origen's menu. The stem cells will come from eggs laid by unmodified pedigree[4] birds, he says. All the same, Origen's website says the company has licenses for tools for genetically engineering birds, and it talks about engineering birds that lay eggs containing medical drugs.

Animal welfare groups say that it would be cruel if breeders used technology to mass-produce the fastest-growing birds. Some birds already go lame when bone growth doesn't keep pace with muscle growth. "The last thing they should be doing is increasing growth

---

[1]pluripotent = able to develop into many different kinds of cells.

[2]donor = person or animal that gives something (in this case, cells).

[3]strains = breeds of animal within one species.

[4]pedigree = pure-bred.

rates," says Abigail Hall of Britain's Royal Society for the Prevention of Cruelty to Animals.

There are other dangers. If one bird were vulnerable to a disease, all its clones would be too. But if one set of clones fell victim to a disease, the technology would allow farmers to "roll out" a resistant set rapidly.

There could also be benefits for consumers, as farmers could quickly adopt strains that don't carry food-poisoning bacteria such as *Salmonella*, for instance. Whether shoppers will buy meat from a clone, even if it's not genetically engineered, remains to be seen. And the FDA has yet to decide whether meat and milk from cloned animals is fit for humans.

Vocabulary

Select the letter of the answer that is closest in meaning to the italicized word or phrase.

1. Factory farming could soon enter a new *era*.
    a. control
    b. age
    c. plan
    d. law

2. Companies are developing the technology needed to clone chickens on a *massive* scale.
    a. famous
    b. huge
    c. small
    d. modern

3. Chicken farms could have birds that all grow at the same *rate*.
    a. speed
    b. slowness
    c. rush
    d. size

4. The *prospect* has alarmed animal welfare groups.
    a. offer
    b. test
    c. idea
    d. preparation

5. Another challenge for the company is to *scale up* production.
    a. discontinue
    b. develop
    c. decrease
    d. increase

6. To do this, the company has *teamed up* with another company.
   a. worked together with   c. put in order
   b. worked in small groups with   d. taken control of

7. The company is now trying to *modify* the machines.
   a. exchange   c. envisage
   b. adapt   d. replace

8. The company *envisages* freezing stem cells.
   a. is not considering   c. is fighting
   b. is planning on   d. is organizing

9. If one bird were *vulnerable to* a disease, all its clones would be too.
   a. without defense against   c. protected from
   b. hurt by   d. free from

10. Farmers could quickly *adopt* strains that don't carry food poisoning bacteria.
    a. take on   c. challenge
    b. object to   d. avoid

Vocabulary Extension

Part A

Match the verbs with the nouns as they were used in the context of the reading. Look back at the reading to check your answers. Add two more nouns that may be used with each adjective.

a. suffering   c. research   e. demand
b. production   d. machines

1. __c__ fund   research _____ _____

2. ____ increase   _____ _____ _____

3. ____ meet   _____ _____ _____

4. ____ scale up   _____ _____ _____

5. ____ modify   _____ _____ _____

Part B

Take turns asking and answering questions about the reading, using the phrases from Part A.

Comprehension

Looking for the Main Ideas

Circle the letter of the best answer to the first question. Write complete answers to the other questions.

1. What is the main idea of the first paragraph?
    a. United States companies plan to clone chickens.
    b. Cloning chickens is the future of chicken farming.
    c. We now have the technology to clone chickens.
    d. Cloning chickens will increase chicken production.

2. Why is it desirable to have chickens that are all identical?

3. Why are animal welfare groups against mass production of chickens?

4. What are the advantages and disadvantages of mass-producing identical chickens?

Skimming and Scanning for Details

Scan the reading to find the answers to these questions. Write complete answers.

1. In paragraph 3, line 4, what does *it* mean?

2. How is a chimera created?

3. What is the difference between a chimera and a clone?

4. How does Origen plan to scale up production of genetically engineered chickens?

5. The first sentence in paragraph 8 refers to "another challenge." What was the first challenge?

6. What discrepancy is noted between information on Origen's web site and statements made by its spokesperson?

Making Inferences and Drawing Conclusions

The answers to these questions are not directly stated in the reading. Write complete answers.

1. Why might some shoppers hesitate to buy meat from cloned chickens?

2. What can you deduce from the article about the motivation of chicken farmers?

3. Why might Origen be unwilling to reveal details of its results?

4. What did you deduce from the article about chicken farming in the United States?

5. Do you think the article presents a balanced view of the topic? What is the author's opinion?

Discussion

Discuss these questions with your classmates.
1. Would you like all chickens to taste the same? Why or why not?
2. Do you think there are purposes for which cloning technology should not be used?
3. What are the benefits of cloning chickens and other farm animals? What are the dangers?

Writing a Summary

Write a one-paragraph summary of Reading 1. Check your summary with the Summary Checklist on page 273.

Paraphrasing

Paraphrase the last paragraph in Reading 2. Look at pages 267–270 to find out about paraphrasing. Begin with "As Graves reports, . . ." or "Based on Graves's article, ..."

Research

Do research to find the name of an organization or group that is against eating meat. Find three arguments for and against the group's point of view. Use the library and the Internet to find facts to support your arguments. Use your own experience and that of your friends to gather information on this topic.

You may use your research later to write an argument essay.

Student Essay

Read the following essay written by a student.

Against Animal Rights

There has been a debate about animal rights for a long time. People who support animal rights believe that animals should have the same rights as humans, such as the right to equality and freedom. It is important that as rational humans we protect all living things in order to keep our planet in balance. However, it is my belief that this does not mean that animals should have the same rights as humans. First, animals are not the same as humans; they are different. If we give them the same rights as humans, we will not be able to eat meat or keep animals for pleasure and entertainment, which humans have done since the beginning of time.

Are animals like us? This is a complex problem. It is true that animals feel pain like humans, but they cannot think like humans. Animals cannot reason. Animals do not survive by making conscious decisions. Human rights are about conscious decisions we make about how we live and how we behave toward one another. Can animals make decisions like that? Animals cannot tell you what their rights are. No animal can take you to court for violating its rights. This does not mean we should treat them cruelly or in a way that is not humane. On the contrary, we should treat them with respect because they are different from us. We need to treat all living species with respect to keep our planet in balance.

Secondly, if animals had the same rights as humans, then people who killed animals for food would be murderers. Anyone who ate a steak or had turkey for Thanksgiving would go to prison. What would happen if someone killed a fly? Most people who support animal rights are vegetarians. They believe that humans are supposed to be vegetarians, and that their teeth and stomachs are designed to eat vegetables and not meat. However, there is historical and biological proof that humans have always eaten meat. They hunted animals for food and ate seeds and nuts. Humans are not different today. Not only could we no longer eat meat, but we could not wear leather or fur. Humans have been wearing the skins of animals since the beginning. If it was not wrong then, why should it be wrong now?

My opponents say it is wrong for people to use animals in experiments or use them for entertainment. The web page of PETA (People for the Ethical Treatment of Animals), an organization that supports animal rights, says, "Animals are not ours to eat, wear, experiment on or use for entertainment." People who support animal rights have such strong beliefs about this that they have set fire to or destroyed fur and leather stores and medical laboratories. They have even used violence to show their beliefs. Is this humane toward other humans? They believe that animals should not be used for research even if it would lead to cures for deadly diseases. Using animals for research has saved and will save human lives, but this does not matter to animal rights supporters. Is it better to experiment on humans rather than animals? They think so. They also believe that animals should not be used for entertainment. This means that we could not have zoos to go to, and we could not even have pets because to have pets would be a form of pleasure and entertainment.

In conclusion, I think people want to protect all species to keep the earth in balance. Some want to give animals the same rights as humans, while others, which I think are the majority, want to give animals the right to be free from cruelty and torture. Even if some animals are more conscious of the world than others, this does not mean animals are "like us." They are different and cannot have the same rights as humans. If they did, we could no longer eat meat, wear their skins, or use them for research. This does not mean we should be cruel to animals. We should respect them and treat them humanely.

Fernando
Brazil

Student Essay Follow-Up

1. Underline the thesis statement.
2. Is the student's argument for animal rights or against them? State his three reasons.
3. Are the two reasons developed in the body paragraphs?
4. Examine paragraph 1. Do all the ideas support the student's opinion?
5. Are the main points restated in the conclusion? Does the writer give a final comment on the topic?

Organizing: The Argument Essay

In an argument essay, just like an oral argument, you must win the person over to your way of thinking. You must appeal to the other person's sense of reason by being logical and by providing evidence.

Assume that the reader does not agree with you. If the reader did agree, then you would not have to write an argument. When arguing your point, remember not to insult the reader in any way just because he or she may have a different opinion than you do. Insulting your reader with a statement such as "People who believe that handguns should not be banned are all killers" will weaken your argument. Always be respectful and logical.

Just presenting your own reasons is not sufficient to convince the reader. In order to convince the reader, you must understand your opponents' position and the reasons they would give to support their opinion. It is therefore essential to know both sides of the argument in order to be convincing.

Exercise 1

Look at both sides of the issue. Read each thesis statement and then write two reasons for it and two reasons against it. The first one is done for you.

1. Is it right to clone animals?

   For

   a. Cloning allows us to mass-produce animals that provide products that are desirable to humans.

   b. It is possible for scientists to advance our knowledge of genetics by studying cloned animals.

   Against

   a. It violates animal rights.

   b. Cloning is expensive. We could spend the money on more important things.

2. Animals should be used for scientific and medical research.

   For

   a. _____
      _____

   b. _____
      _____

   Against

   a. _____
      _____

   b. _____
      _____

3. It is a good idea to genetically engineer farm animals and fish for consumption.

      For   *Against*

a. _____   a. _____

    _____   _____

b. _____   b. _____

    _____   _____

4. It is not right to kill animals for any reason.

      For   *Against*

a. _____   a. _____

    _____   _____

b. _____   b. _____

    _____   _____

Using Specific Evidence

Nothing will support your opinion better than pertinent facts and statistics. To find evidence, go to the library, where you will find facts, numbers, and data. These will make your argument more definite and harder to contest.

Look at the following examples of statements with and without support:

Examples:

Without support: Many Americans don't support human cloning.

With support: According to the 2002 Genetics and Public Policy Center survey, most Americans (76 percent) oppose allowing scientists to work on ways to clone humans.

Without support: Most Americans support giving animals the same rights as people.

With support: According to a 2003 Gallup News Service poll, 71 percent of Americans said animals deserved some protection, and a full 25 percent responded that animals deserve the same rights as people.

Use authority to support your argument. The authority you use must be recognized, reliable, and expert. In the above examples, the authority for cloning was the Genetics and Public Policy Center, and the authority for animal rights was the Gallup News Service, a famous polling service.

When using an authority, you should identify it by name and enclose the exact words of the authority in quotation marks. In Reading 2, an authority is used to make a convincing argument:

> "The last thing they should be doing is increasing growth rates," says Abigail Hall of Britain's Royal Society for the Prevention of Cruelty to Animals.

Avoid vague references to authorities using terms such as "authorities agree . . . ," "people say . . . ," and "research says . . . ." These are not acceptable in a logical argument.

Exercise 2

Which of these sentences do not use a reliable authority?

1. A 2002 poll from Johns Hopkins University shows that 76 percent of Americans are against scientific efforts to clone humans.

2. Research indicates that most Americans are against cloning humans.

3. A recent study shows that fish don't like fishermen.

4. According to PETA (People for the Ethical Treatment of Animals), fish farms make fish suffer by keeping them in overcrowded conditions.

Organizing Your Argument

The Introduction

Introduce the topic by giving background information. It is important that the reader understand the issue to be argued. Define any terms that are unclear. If you were going to argue against animal testing, you would have to define animal testing very clearly before taking your stand.

The thesis statement in an argument essay is different from those in other types of essays. In the argument essay thesis, you have to be persuasive and take a stand or choose a side on an issue. Look back at the thesis statement of the student essay.

Body Paragraphs

The body paragraphs give reasons for your opinion and support them with evidence or facts. Each body paragraph relates back to a point of the argument stated in your thesis. The body paragraphs should be ordered so that the strongest reason is last.

A characteristic of the argument essay is that it recognizes the opposing view and proves it wrong, or *refutes* it. This means that you start with one of your opponents' viewpoints and use your superior reasons to prove that it is wrong. Generally, the refutation occurs in the last body paragraph. Look back at the student essay to see how the student refutes the opposing argument.

Read the following argument about animal testing. Then read the sample refutation.

Argument

Using animals for testing is wrong and should be banned. Animals feel pain in the same way as humans. Causing pain to an animal is the same as causing pain to a human being. If animals have the same right to be free from pain, we should not experiment on them. Each year in the United States, about 70 million animals are used in research. They are tortured, injured, and killed in the name of science by private companies, government agencies, and educational institutions. Animals are used to test the degree of harmfulness of certain household products and their ingredients. Sometimes animals are injected with infectious diseases such as AIDS. In most cases, the animals are left to die with no certainty that this suffering and death will save a single life or benefit humans in any way at all. There is no reason to make innocent animals suffer; other alternatives should be used.

Refutation

While it is true that many animals suffer and die in scientific research, it is a fact that we need animal research for advances in medicine and product safety. Most of today's medical advances, such as vaccines, surgical procedures, and so on, would not have been possible without animal experimentation. Computer models or artificial substances cannot work in the same way as blood, bones, or organs can in a living system. It is not possible to predict the course of many diseases or the effects of treatments without testing them on living systems. At present, scientists do not know enough about living systems to replicate one on a computer. Until that day comes, animals are vital in research if medical progress is to continue.

The Conclusion

In the conclusion, summarize the main points of your argument or restate the thesis. End your conclusion with a strong statement, such as a demand for action or an alternative solution.

The following is a brief outline for an argument essay:

Introduction

Background information
Thesis: Take a stand

Paragraph 1

Argument that supports your opinion

Paragraph 2

Stronger argument that supports your opinion

Paragraph 3

Strongest argument that supports your opinion

Paragraph 4

Refutation

Conclusion

Restate thesis or summarize main points.

End with an alternative or demand for action.

Writing Practice

Choose one of the following topics.

1. Write an argument for or against eating meat, using the information you researched earlier in this chapter.
2. Write an argument for or against using animals for medical research.
3. Write an argument for or against using animals for entertainment.
4. Write an argument for or against fish farms.

1. **Pre-writing.**

   Work alone, with a partner, or in a group.

   a. Brainstorm the topic. Look at page 258 to find out about brainstorming. Write three reasons for and three reasons against some aspect of the topic.
   b. Select the strongest points. Which side do you want to take a stand on?
   c. Work on a thesis statement.

2. **Develop an outline.**

   a. Organize your ideas.
      Step 1: Write your thesis statement, including the three reasons for or against some aspect of the topic.
      Step 2: Order your reasons. Choose the opponents' arguments that you will refute.
      Step 3: Decide what kinds of support would be relevant. Go to the library or use the Internet to get relevant facts.
   b. Make a more detailed outline. The essay outline on page 22 will help you.

3. **Write a rough draft.**

4. **Revise your rough draft.**

   Use the checklist on page 262.

5. Edit your essay.

> Check your work for correct use of transition words.

> **Example:**

>> *Error:* Some people want to save animals from cruelty and torture, instead others want to give animals the same rights as humans.

>> *Correct:* Although some people want to save animals from cruelty and torture, others want to give animals the same rights as humans.

> Look at page 263 for symbols to use when editing your work.

6. Write your final copy.

Video Activity • Better Lives for Chickens

1. The video describes a chicken farm in Colorado where the chickens are not kept in cages. Do you think animals have rights? Would you be willing to pay $1 more for a dozen eggs from a humane chicken farm? Why or why not?

2. Review these words used in the video: *roost* (verb), *rafters* (noun), *ban* (verb), *hare-brained* (adjective).

3. After you watch the video, read the following statements and circle each correct answer.

   a. The chickens in the video cannot _____.

         roost in rafters   stretch their wings   fly away   socialize

   b. The chicken farm in the video is home to _____ chickens.

         5,500   6,500   55,000   75,000

   c. Some _____ countries have already banned cages for chickens.

         small   European   tropical   Asian

   d. The natural egg business has climbed _____ in the last year, according to the video.

         100 percent   200 percent   300 percent   tremendously

   e. Chickens that are not in cages produce _____ eggs than chickens in cages.

         bigger   fewer   more   smaller

4. Do you think the humane chicken farm is a "hare-brained scheme" or a good business plan? Why or why not? Explain in a journal entry or a persuasive composition.

Internet Activity

- Go to the web site of a well-known British or American news magazine or newspaper. Find a recent news article on the topic of animal rights. Summarize the article in about 50 words. Tell your class about the information you found.

- What web sites did you use for your search? Which ones were most helpful? Did you encounter any problems when searching for this information? How did you solve them?

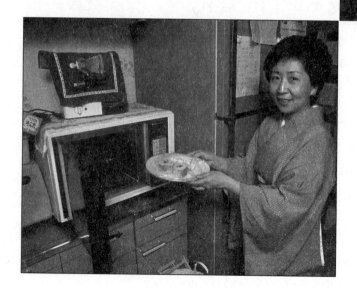

CHAPTER NINE

Readings from Literature

Pre-Reading Questions

Discuss these questions.

1. Look at the picture. What is traditional and what is not traditional?
2. How have traditional ways of preparing food changed?
3. Which kind of food do you prefer to eat—freshly prepared food or pre-packaged and ready-to-eat food?

Activity

1. Decide whether the following phrases are more likely to be said by a young adult or a parent, and put them in the proper column in the table.

   Why don't you eat your vegetables?

   Clean up your room!

   Why don't we meet your friend?

   I don't have time to go with you.

   I'd like to buy my own.

   It's time you thought about the future.

   That is so corny!

   Then add some phrases of your own.

Parent	Young Adult

2. Discuss these questions with your classmates.
   a. What kind of things do your parents tell you to do?
   b. If your parents have different ideas or values than you do, how do you react?

3. How are your ideas different from your parents' ideas? Make short notes in the following categories:

	My Ideas	My Parents' Ideas
Education		
Marriage		
Work		
Responsibility		
Other		

Winterblossom Garden

by David Low

The following is an excerpt from an autobiographical short story. Born in 1952 in Queens, New York, David Low now lives in the East Village of New York City. The short story "Winterblossom Garden" appeared in the anthology Under Western Eyes *(Doubleday, New York, 1995), edited by Garrett Hongo.*

My mother pours two cups of tea from the porcelain teapot that has always been in its wicker basket[1] on the kitchen table. On the sides of the teapot, a maiden[2] dressed in a jade-green gown visits a bearded emperor at his palace near the sky. The maiden waves a vermilion[3] fan.

"I bet you still don't know how to cook," my mother says. She places a plate of steamed roast pork buns before me.

"Mom, I'm not hungry."

"If you don't eat more, you will get sick."

I take a bun from the plate, but it is too hot. My mother hands me a napkin so I can put the bun down. Then she peels a banana in front of me.

"I'm not obsessed with food like you," I say.

"What's wrong with eating?"

She looks at me as she takes a big bite of the banana.

"I'm going to have a photography show at the end of the summer."

"Are you still taking pictures of old buildings falling down? How ugly! Why don't you take happier pictures?"

"I thought you would want to come," I answer. "It's not easy to get a gallery."

"If you were married," she says, her voice becoming unusually soft, "you would take better pictures. You would be happy."

---

[1]wicker basket = basket made of woven grass or twigs.

[2]maiden = young unmarried woman (old English).

[3]vermilion = bright red.

"I don't know what you mean. Why do you think getting married will make me happy?"

My mother looks at me as if I have spoken in Serbo-Croatian. She always gives me this look when I say something she does not want to hear. She finishes the banana; then she puts the plate of food away. Soon she stands at the sink, turns on the hot water and washes dishes. My mother learned long ago that silence has a power of its own.

She takes out a blue cookie tin from the dining room cabinet. Inside this tin, my mother keeps her favorite photographs. Whenever I am ready to leave, my mother brings it to the living room and opens it on the coffee table. She knows I cannot resist looking at these pictures again; I will sit down next to her on the sofa for at least another hour. Besides the portraits of the family, my mother has images of people I have never met: her father, who owned a poultry store on Pell Street and didn't get a chance to return to China before he died; my father's younger sister, who still runs a pharmacy in Rio de Janeiro (she sends the family an annual supply of cough drops); my mother's cousin Kay, who died at thirty, a year after she came to New York from Hong Kong. Although my mother has a story to tell for each photograph, she refuses to speak at all about Kay, as if the mere mention of her name will bring back her ghost to haunt us all.

My mother always manages to find a picture I have not seen before; suddenly I discover I have a relative who is a mortician[4] in Vancouver. I pick up a portrait of Uncle Lao-Hu, a silver-haired man with a goatee[5] who owned a curio shop on Mott Street until he retired last year and moved to Hawaii. In a color print, he stands in the doorway of his store, holding a bamboo Moon Man in front of him, as if it were a bowling trophy. The statue, which is actually two feet tall, has a staff in its left hand, while its right palm balances a peach, a sign of long life. The top of the Moon Man's head protrudes in the shape of an eggplant; my mother believes that such a head contains an endless wealth of wisdom.

"Your uncle Lao-Hu is a wise man, too," my mother says, "except when he's in love. When he still owned the store, he fell in love with his women customers all the time. He was always losing money because he gave away his merchandise to any woman who smiled at him."

I see my uncle's generous arms full of gifts: a silver Buddha, an ivory dragon, a pair of emerald chopsticks.

---

[4]mortician = person whose job is to take care of funerals; also called an undertaker.

[5]goatee = small pointed beard.

"These women confused him," she adds. "That's what happens when a Chinese man doesn't get married."

Mother shakes her head and sighs.

"In his last letter, Lao-Hu invited me to visit him in Honolulu. Your father refuses to leave the store."

"Why don't you go anyway?"

"I can't leave your father alone." She stares at the pictures scattered on the coffee table.

"Mom, why don't you do something for yourself? I thought you were going to start taking English lessons."

"Your father thinks it would be a waste of time."

While my mother puts the cookie tin away, I stand up to stretch my legs. I gaze at a photograph that hangs on the wall above the sofa: my parents' wedding picture. My mother was matched[6] to my father; she claims that if her own father had been able to repay the money that Dad spent to bring her to America, she might never have married him at all. In the wedding picture she wears a stunned expression. She is dressed in a luminous gown of ruffles[7] and lace; the train[8] spirals at her feet. As she clutches the bouquet tightly against her stomach, she might be asking, "What am I doing? Who is this man?" My father's face is thinner than it is now. His tuxedo[9] is too small for him; the flower in his lapel[10] droops. He hides his hand with the crooked pinky behind his back.

I have never been sure if my parents really love each other. I have only seen them kiss at their children's weddings. They never touch each other in public. When I was little, I often thought they went to sleep in the clothes they wore to work.

---

[6]matched =given in an arranged marriage.

[7]ruffles = decorative frills on clothing, usually found around the neck, wrist, or hem.

[8]train = long back part of a dress that trails along the ground.

[9]tuxedo = formal suit worn by men.

[10]lapel = part of the front of a coat or jacket that is attached to the collar and folds back on both sides.

Vocabulary

Select the letter of the answer that is closest in meaning to the italicized word or phrase.

1. His mother is *obsessed with* food.
    a. has problems with
    c. thinks about all the time
    b. never thinks about
    d. criticizes all the time

2. He cannot *resist* looking at the pictures.
   a. force himself to   c. accept
   b. stop himself from   d. insist on

3. His uncle held the Moon Man in front of him as if it were a *trophy*.
   a. flower   c. child
   b. prize   d. puppet

4. The statue's head *protrudes* in the shape of an eggplant.
   a. sticks out   c. gets smaller
   b. hangs down   d. sinks

5. He *gazes at* a photograph on the wall.
   a. talks about   c. points to
   b. mentions   d. looks at for a long time

6. She has a *stunned* expression.
   a. doubtful   c. clear
   b. surprised   d. positive

7. His mother is dressed in a *luminous* wedding gown.
   a. white   c. plain
   b. heavy   d. shiny

8. She *clutches* a bouquet against her stomach.
   a. holds tightly   c. shows
   b. opens up   d. hides

9. The flower in his lapel *droops*.
   a. looks fresh   c. hangs down
   b. shines   d. sticks out

10. He hides his hand with the crooked *pinky*.
    a. nail   c. thumb
    b. little finger   d. middle finger

Vocabulary Extension

Part A

Read the list of verbs below. Find verbs in the reading that have the same meaning.

1. manage   <u>run</u>

2. revive   _____

3. abandon   _____

4. stare   _____

5. hold tightly   _____

6. conceal   _____

Part B

Use the verbs you found in Part A to complete these questions.

1. Why is his mother _____ a bouquet in the picture?

2. Why doesn't she want to _____ his father?

3. What does the son think as he _____ at the wedding picture?

4. Why does the father _____ his pinky?

5. What kind of store does his cousin _____?

6. What does the mother think will _____ the aunt's ghost?

With a partner, take turns asking and answering these questions.

Comprehension

Understanding the Story

1. Describe the sequence of events in the story.

2. What information does the son tell his mother?

3. How does the mother respond?

4. What does the son want his mother to do? Why?

5. What does the mother want her son to do? Why?

Interpreting the Story

1. How do the actions of the people in the story express their values and feelings? Give examples.

2. Why is the blue cookie tin important both to the son and to the mother?

3. What is the mother's idea of marriage? How might this be different from the son's idea?

Understanding the Characters

1. Describe the character of the mother. What are her values? Support your description with examples from the story.

2. Describe the character of the son. What are his values? Support your description with examples from the story.

3. Role play the conversation between the writer and his mother. Continue the conversation with your own ideas.

Recognizing Style

1. From whose point of view is the story told? Does the writer want us to sympathize with or criticize this point of view?

2. Think about how the following images are used in the story. What do they symbolize?
   a. The teapot
   b. The blue cookie tin
   c. The parents' wedding picture

3. Find examples of similes and metaphors in the story. How do they help us to understand the characters?

Discussion

Discuss these questions with your classmates.
1. What are some things that parents and children have different ideas about?
2. Do you think parents are usually right?
3. If you were a parent, what advice would you give your child?
4. If your values and your parents' values were different, how would this affect your relationship with them?
5. What advice would you give to the mother and son in the story?

Mrs. Sen's

by Jhumpa Lahiri

The following is an excerpt from a short story by Jhumpa Lahiri. Born in London in 1967 and raised in Rhode Island, the daughter of Bengali parents, Lahiri has a heritage and culture influenced by both India and the United States. "Mrs. Sen's" appeared in her collection of short stories entitled The Interpreter of Maladies *(Houghton Mifflin, Boston, 1999).*

Eliot didn't mind going to Mrs. Sen's after school. By September the tiny beach house where he and his mother lived year-round was already cold; Eliot and his mother had to bring a portable heater along whenever they moved from one room to another, and to seal the windows with plastic sheets and a hair dryer. The beach was barren and dull to play on alone; the only neighbors who stayed on past Labor Day, a young married couple, had no children, and Eliot no longer found it interesting to gather broken mussel shells in his bucket, or to stroke the seaweed, strewn like strips of emerald lasagna on the sand. Mrs. Sen's apartment was warm, sometimes too warm; the radiators continuously hissed like a pressure cooker. Eliot learned to remove his sneakers first thing in Mrs. Sen's doorway, and to place them on the bookcase next to a row of Mrs. Sen's slippers, each a different color, with soles as flat as cardboard and a ring of leather to hold her big toe.

He especially enjoyed watching Mrs. Sen as she chopped things, seated on newspapers on the living room floor. Instead of a knife she used a blade that curved like the prow[1] of a Viking ship, sailing to battle in distant seas. The blade was hinged at one end to a narrow wooden base. The steel, more black than silver, lacked a uniform polish, and had a serrated[2] crest, she told Eliot, for grating. Each afternoon Mrs. Sen lifted the blade and locked it into place, so that it met the base at an angle. Facing the sharp edge without ever touching it, she took whole vegetables between her hands and hacked them apart: cauliflower, cabbage, butternut squash. She split things in half, then quarters, speedily producing florets, cubes, slices, and shreds. She could peel a potato in seconds. At times she sat cross-legged, at times with legs splayed, surrounded by an array of colanders[3] and shallow bowls of water in which she immersed her chopped ingredients.

While she worked she kept an eye on the television and an eye on Eliot, but she never seemed to keep an eye on the blade. Nevertheless she refused to let Eliot walk around when she was chopping. "Just sit, sit please, it will take just two more minutes," she said, pointing to the sofa, which was draped at all times with a green and black bedcover printed with rows of elephants bearing palanquins on their backs. The daily procedure took about an hour. In order to occupy Eliot she supplied him with the comics section of the newspaper, and crackers spread with peanut butter, and sometimes a Popsicle, or carrot sticks sculpted with her blade. She would have roped off the area if she could. Once, though, she broke her own rule; in need of additional supplies, and reluctant to rise from the catastrophic mess that barricaded her, she asked Eliot to fetch something from the kitchen. "If you don't mind, there is a plastic bowl, large enough to hold this spinach, in the cabinet next to the fridge. Careful, oh dear, be careful," she cautioned as he approached. "Just leave it, thank you, on the coffee table, I can reach."

She had brought the blade from India, where apparently there was at least one in every household. "Whenever there is a wedding in the family," she told Eliot one day, "or a large celebration of any kind, my mother sends out word in the evening for all the neighborhood women to bring blades just like this one, and then they sit in an enormous circle on the roof of our building, laughing and gossiping and slicing fifty kilos of vegetables through the night." Her profile hovered protectively

---

[1]prow = front part of a boat, which on some old ships curved up quite far.
[2]serrated = jagged.
[3]colander = a metal or plastic bowl with holes in it, used to separate liquid from food.

over her work, a confetti of cucumber, eggplant, and onion skins heaped around her. "It is impossible to fall asleep those nights, listening to their chatter." She paused to look at a pine tree framed by the living room window. "Here, in this place where Mr. Sen has brought me, I cannot sometimes sleep in so much silence."

Another day she sat prying the pimpled yellow fat off chicken parts, then dividing them between thigh and leg. As the bones cracked apart over the blade her golden bangles jostled[4], her forearms glowed, and she exhaled audibly[5] through her nose. At one point she paused, gripping the chicken with both hands, and stared out the window. Fat and sinew clung to her fingers.

"Eliot, if I began to scream right now at the top of my lungs, would someone come?"

"Mrs. Sen, what's wrong?"

"Nothing. I am only asking if someone would come."

Eliot shrugged. "Maybe."

"At home that is all you have to do. Not everybody has a telephone. But just raise your voice a bit, or express grief or joy of any kind, and one whole neighborhood and half of another has come to share the news, to help with arrangements."

By then Eliot understood that when Mrs. Sen said home, she meant India, not the apartment where she sat chopping vegetables. He thought of his own home, just five miles away, and the young married couple who waved from time to time as they jogged at sunset along the shore. On Labor Day they'd had a party. People were piled[6] on the deck, eating, drinking, the sound of their laughter rising above the weary sigh[7] of the waves. Eliot and his mother weren't invited. It was one of the rare days his mother had off, but they didn't go anywhere. She did the laundry, and balanced the checkbook, and, with Eliot's help, vacuumed the inside of the car. Eliot had suggested that they go through the car wash a few miles down the road as they did every now and then, so that they could sit inside, safe and dry, as soap and water and a circle of giant canvas ribbons slapped[8] the windshield, but his mother said she was too tired, and sprayed the car with a hose. When, by evening, the crowd on the neighbors' deck began dancing, she

---

[4]jostled = pushed against each other.

[5]exhaled audibly = breathed out noisily.

[6]piled = crowded.

[7]weary sigh = heavy, tired sound.

[8]slapped = hit.

looked up their number in the phone book and asked them to keep it down.

"They might call you," Eliot said eventually to Mrs. Sen. "But they might complain that you were making too much noise."

From where Eliot sat on the sofa he could detect her curious scent of mothballs and cumin, and he could see the perfectly centered part in her braided hair, which was shaded with crushed vermilion and therefore appeared to be blushing. At first Eliot had wondered if she had cut her scalp, or if something had bitten here there. But then one day he saw her standing before the bathroom mirror, solemnly applying, with the head of a thumbtack, a fresh stroke of scarlet powder, which she stored in a small jam jar. A few grains of the powder fell onto the bridge of her nose as she used the thumbtack to stamp a dot above her eyebrows. "I must wear the powder every day," she explained when Eliot asked her what it was for, "for the rest of the days that I am married."

"Like a wedding ring, you mean?"

"Exactly, Eliot, exactly like a wedding ring. Only with no fear of losing it in the dishwater."

Vocabulary

Select the letter of the answer that is closest in meaning to the italicized word or phrase.

1. The beach was *barren.*
   a. dirty
   b. polluted
   c. empty
   d. rainy

2. The seaweed was *strewn* like strips of emerald lasagna.
   a. spread around
   b. lost
   c. collected
   d. growing

3. Eliot placed his sneakers next to *a row of* Mrs. Sen's slippers.
   a. a group of
   b. a line of
   c. a circle of
   d. a mass of

4. Instead of a knife Mrs. Sen used *a blade.*
   a. an old-fashioned fork
   b. the cutting part of a knife
   c. the top part of a hammer
   d. the pointed part of a piece of wood

5. She took whole vegetables between her hands and *hacked* them apart.
   a. cut roughly
   b. cut carefully
   c. cut thinly
   d. pulled quickly

6. She was surrounded by *an array* of colanders.
   a. a variety
   b. a pair
   c. a copy
   d. a crowd

7. She was surrounded by shallow bowls of water in which she *immersed* her chopped ingredients.
   a. put underwater
   b. dried for a long time
   c. stored for a time
   d. salted

8. The sofa was *draped* at all times with a bedcover.
   a. organized
   b. decorated
   c. fresh
   d. covered

9. She was *reluctant* to rise from the mess.
   a. excited
   b. happy
   c. unwilling
   d. bored

10. Eliot could *detect* her curious scent.
    a. imagine
    b. notice
    c. experience
    d. value

Vocabulary Extension

Part A

Match the verbs with the nouns as they were used in the context of the reading. Look back at the reading to check your answers. Add two more nouns that may be used with each verb.

a. a potato   c. the noise   e. shells
b. your voice   d. vegetables

1. _e_ gather   _shells_   _____   _____

2. ___ chop   _____ _____   _____

3. ___ peel   _____ _____   _____

4. ___ raise   _____ _____   _____

5. ___ keep down   _____ _____   _____

Part B

Make questions about the reading, using verb and noun combinations from Part A.

1. Why does Eliot _____ _____ on the beach?

2. How does Mrs. Sen like to _____ _____?

3. How does Mrs. Sen _____ _____?

4. What would happen if Mrs. Sen _____ _____?

5. Why would the neighbors ask her to _____ _____?

With a partner, take turns asking and answering these questions.

Comprehension

Understanding the Story

Discuss these questions with a classmate.

1. Why does Eliot go to Mrs. Sen's house every day?
2. What does Eliot do at Mrs. Sen's house?
3. What differences does Eliot notice between Mrs. Sen's home and his own home? Make a list in the chart below.

Mrs. Sen's home	Eliot's home

Interpreting the Story

Answer the following questions. Support your answers with sentences from the story.

1. How does Eliot feel when he is with his mother?
2. What kind of home life does he have?
3. How does Eliot feel when he is at Mrs. Sen's?
4. How old do you think Eliot is?
5. How is the meaning of the word *home* different for Eliot and for Mrs. Sen?

Understanding the Characters

Discuss these questions with a classmate. Support your answers with sentences from the story.

1. What values are important to Mrs. Sen?
2. What values are important to Eliot's mother?

3. Make up a conversation between Mrs. Sen and Eliot's mother. What would they agree about? What would they disagree about?

Recognizing Style

Discuss these questions with a classmate.

1. From whose point of view is the story told? Is this different from the author's point of view? How does the narrator's point of view become apparent?
2. Think about how the following images are used in the story. What do they symbolize?
   a. The chopping blade
   b. The car wash
   c. The scarlet powder
3. Find examples of similes and metaphors in the story. How do they help to convey images?

Examples:

Simile: The seaweed was strewn like strips of emerald lasagna.
Metaphor: The weary sigh of the waves.

Discussion

Discuss these questions with a classmate.

1. Whom do you sympathize more with in the story, Eliot or Mrs. Sen? Why?
2. What do you think will happen at the end of the story?
3. What are some everyday things that are done differently in your culture than in the American culture or another culture that you know?
4. Which culture would you prefer to live in: a culture in which people are close to each other and material things are not important or a culture in which independence, privacy, and money are important? Give reasons.

Narrator and Point of View

Usually, when we ask someone what his or her point of view is, we are asking about the person's opinion. When we are discussing literature, however, *point of view* means the perspective of the person who is telling the story. The story can be presented through the eyes of a character or through the eyes of the author, or the point of view can alternate between characters or between the author and characters. The author can choose from a number of different options.

First-Person Narrator

The story of "Winterblossom Garden" is told in the first person. This means that we only know what is going on in the mind of the narrator. We only know about events that he sees or experiences. We don't know what his mother thinks, though we can guess by trying to interpret her actions and words. The first-person point of view can be used to increase suspense, because some information can be hidden from readers and then used to surprise them later. It can also create empathy as we try to identify and understand the narrator's feelings. On the other hand, we may come to dislike or distrust the narrator, and in this case we may notice a gap between what the narrator says and what the author wants us to think.

Third-Person Narrator

A story told in the third person refers to all characters as "she," "he," or "they," not as "I." But here there is also a choice for the writer. The author can write as an "omniscient," or all-knowing, narrator who sees everything. In this case, the author is not restricted as to time or location and can see everything that goes on in all the characters' minds. Or the author can write from a limited third person point of view. In this case, the story is limited to the thoughts of a major character, and nothing is described in the story unless it is seen, felt, or experienced by this character. Look at the excerpt from "Mrs. Sen's." Is it told by an omniscient narrator or by a limited third-person narrator?

1. Rewrite the following excerpt from the point of view of a third-person narrator. How does the feeling of the story change?

   My mother always manages to find a picture I have not seen before; suddenly I discover I have a relative who is a mortician in Vancouver. I pick up a portrait of Uncle Lao-Hu.

2. Rewrite the following excerpt from the point of view of a first-person narrator. How does the feeling of the story change?

Eliot didn't mind going to Mrs. Sen's after school. By September the tiny beach house where he and his mother lived year-round was already cold; Eliot and his mother had to bring a portable heater along whenever they moved from one room to another, and to seal the windows with plastic sheets and a hair dryer.

3. Think of an event that happened in your childhood. Write one or two sentences describing what happened in the first person. Then rewrite the sentences in the third person. Read each set of sentences aloud to a partner. How does the feeling of the story change?

Student Essay

Read the following essay written by a student.

The Narrator's Point of View in "Winterblossom Garden" and "Mrs. Sen's"

"Winterblossom Garden" describes the relationship between an adult son and his mother. It is told in the first person, through the eyes of the son. He and his mother have different views of life, not only because of their age difference, but also because she was born in China and he was born and brought up in the United States. "Mrs. Sen's" describes the life of an Indian woman living in the United States who looks after a young boy while his mother is at work. It is told in the third person. The story presents their different understandings of the word "home." Both stories use the narrator's point of view to present the reader with multiple viewpoints on the meaning of home, family, and culture.

Both "Winterblossom Garden" and "Mrs. Sen's" are told through the eyes of one major character. "Winterblossom Garden" is told in the first person, by the character of the son. He describes himself and his feelings directly: "I have never been sure if my parents really love each other." He describes his mother through her actions and her words: "Soon she stands at the sink, turns on the hot water and washes dishes. My mother learned long ago that silence has a power of its own." By using the first-person point of view, the author helps us to identify with the feelings of the son. We try to understand why the son feels so distant from his mother and why there is a gap between them that makes it difficult to communicate. The author presents the son's point of view in a way that also asks us to challenge and criticize him, and to understand his mother's feelings too.

"Mrs. Sen's" is told in the third person, but the point of view is limited to the thoughts and actions of one main character, the boy Eliot. He is curious about Mrs. Sen's home and we observe her life through Eliot's eyes as he notices things that seem magical and mysterious to him: "He especially enjoyed watching Mrs. Sen as she chopped things, seated on newspapers on the living room floor. Instead of a knife she used a blade that curved like the prow of a Viking ship, sailing to battle in distant seas." By the end of the story, we find that we are viewing Mrs. Sen's home more positively than Eliot's. Although Eliot does not complain about his home life, as readers we can see that his life is lonely and cold: "By September the tiny beach house where he and his mother lived year-round was already cold. . . . The beach was barren and dull to play on alone; the only neighbors who stayed on past Labor Day, a young married couple, had no children." The author leaves the reader to come to this conclusion about Eliot's loneliness; she does not state it directly. Using the third person to present Eliot's point of view creates a distance between the narrator and the events being described. It allows the reader to view the events from different perspectives: Eliot's, Mrs. Sen's, Eliot's mother's, and the reader's own.

In conclusion, although "Winterblossom Garden" is told in the first person and "Mrs. Sen's" from a limited third-person point of view, both stories present the reader with many different perspectives. As readers we try to understand the main characters' feelings, but at the same time, we also criticize them and reach our own conclusions. In this way, the reader is also encouraged to examine his or her own culture from a new perspective.

Student Essay Follow-Up

1. Underline the thesis statement.
2. What are the similarities in the use of point of view in these two stories? What are the differences?
3. Can you find any additional points of similarity or difference?

Write your own interpretation of one of the stories in this chapter. Choose one of the following essay assignments.

1. "Winterblossom Garden" illustrates the gap between two generations, but also their need to communicate. Discuss.
2. How does the author of "Mrs. Sen's" make the reader examine his or her own culture from a critical viewpoint?
3. The voice of the narrator in "Mrs. Sen's" is both naïve and wise. Discuss.
4. In "Winterblossom Garden," we understand more from what is not said than from what is said by the characters. Discuss.
5. Compare the character of the son in "Winterblossom Garden" and the character of Eliot in "Mrs. Sen's." How are they similar? How are they different?

1. Pre-writing.

    Work alone, with a partner, or in a group.
    a. Brainstorm the topic. Use one of the techniques on pages 258–260.
    b. Select the most interesting points.
    c. Work on a thesis statement.

2. Develop an outline.

    a. Organize your ideas.
        Step 1: Write your thesis statement.
        Step 2: Organize your points in a logical order.
        Step 3: Find sentences in the story to support your points.
    b. Make a more detailed outline.

3. Write a rough draft.

4. Revise your rough draft.

    Use the Revision Checklist on page 262.

5. Edit your essay.

    Use the editing symbols on page 263.

6. Write your final copy.

Video Activity • The New Globe Theatre

1. The video describes the rebuilding of the Globe Theatre in London, where Shakespeare's plays were performed. What are some famous plays by Shakespeare? Why do you think his works are still performed?

2. Review the following words used in the video: *rubbish* (noun), *glittering* (adjective), *rowdy* (adjective).

3. After you watch the video, do the following exercise. Match the people on the left with the descriptions on the right. Put the correct letter on the line in front of each name.

    ____ 1. Sam Wanamaker   a. went to the original Globe Theatre

    ____ 2. William Shakespeare   b. shut down the Globe in 1642.

    ____ 3. King Lear   c. wanted to build a new Globe.

    ____ 4. Queen Elizabeth I   d. was the greatest Western playwright.

    ____ 5. The Puritans   e. was the title character of one of Shakespeare's plays.

4. What are some features of the Globe Theatre that make it different from most theaters today?

5. Discuss with a group: Why do people enjoy going to the theater? How is it different from going to the cinema? Write a paragraph explaining why people enjoy watching plays and films and say which you prefer and why.

Internet Activity

- Use the Internet to find out about these contemporary writers: Sandra Cisneros, Amy Tan, Alice Walker, Edwidge Dandicat. What do they have in common?

- Choose a book by one of these authors that you would like to read. Tell the class the title of the book and why you want to read it.

Resources
for Writers

How to Get Ideas, Draft, Revise, and Edit

Getting Ideas

Before starting to write on a specific topic, it is important to develop some ideas. In this section, you will learn a number of strategies for generating ideas. These techniques are useful when you first start thinking about your topic and at other times when you find you have nothing to say about a topic.

Brainstorming

To get ideas and stimulate your thoughts, you can use the strategy of **brainstorming.** You can brainstorm alone or with a group.

These are some guidelines to follow when brainstorming:

- Give yourself or the group a limited amount of time.
- Write down the word or phrase you need to get ideas about.
- Write down all the ideas that come to mind. Do not organize your ideas in any way.
- When your time is up, look over the ideas to see if any can be grouped together.

The following is an example of the ideas that came up in a brainstorming session on the subject of video games for children.

Video Games

addictive	fun
time-consuming	more exciting than T.V.
bad for eyes	too violent
expensive	take time away from homework

Since there are more negative than positive points written down, the student might want to write about the negative sides of video games.

Clustering

Clustering is another way of generating ideas. To cluster, you make a visual plan of the connections among your ideas.

Use the following guidelines for clustering:

- Write your topic in the center of your paper and circle it.
- Write an idea related to the topic, circle that idea, and from it draw a line back to the topic. Keep writing down ideas, making circles around them, and connecting them back to the ideas they came from.
- When you have no more ideas, look at your clusters and decide which ideas seem most important.

The following is an example of the ideas that came up in clustering on the subject of obesity. From this diagram, the writer could develop an essay on the causes or effects of obesity.

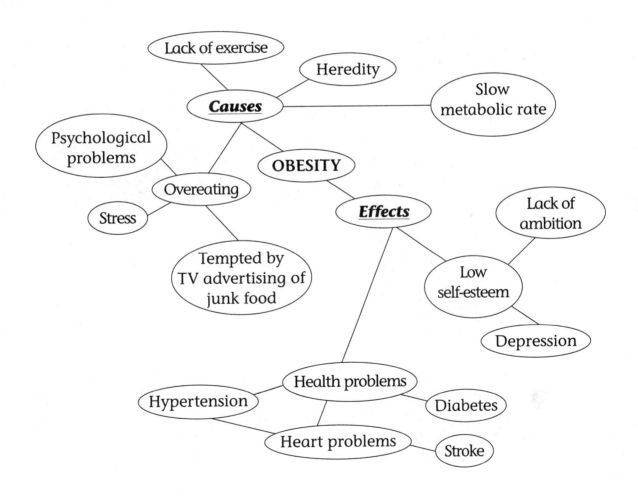

Freewriting

With the **freewriting** technique, you write freely on a topic without stopping. You don't worry about correct grammar or whether what you think is important enough to write down. After you freewrite, you can decide which of your ideas could be useful.

These are some guidelines to follow when freewriting:

- Give yourself a time limit.
- Write the topic at the top of your paper.
- Write as much as you can about the topic. Do not worry about grammar, spelling, organization, or relevance.
- Write until your time is up.
- Read your freewriting and underline the main idea(s).
- Repeat the process, this time using a main idea as your freewriting topic.

The following is an example of the freewriting technique applied to the subject of a vegetarian diet.

A Vegetarian Diet

I am not a vegetarian but two of my friends are. They always tell me how cruel it is to kill animals, and I tell them I need meat to get my protein. They tell me you can get protein from sources other than animal products. <u>Animal products contain fat which can be bad for health, whereas plants are high in fiber and good for health.</u> Even if it were good for me, I just think vegetarian food is boring. But they proved me wrong when I went out to eat with them. <u>The vegetarian dishes were very tasty and there were so many varieties.</u> There are so many cookbooks now for vegetarians I noticed.

The writer has underlined two ideas that could be explored further. These are "Animal products contain fat which can be bad for health, whereas plants are high in fiber and good for health," and "The vegetarian dishes were tasty and there were so many varieties." The writer can take one of these ideas and freewrite about it again.

Drafting

After you have developed some ideas for your essay, it is time to start drafting, or actually writing your essay.

First, you should draft the thesis statement. The thesis statement must tell the reader the main idea you will be discussing and your approach to the main idea. A thesis statement should not simply state what you are going to do—for example, "In this essay I will describe my brother." It should present your approach to the main idea, as in "My brother is both an ambitious and a sociable character." The words *ambitious* and *sociable* make clear the focus of your description of your brother. You might write one paragraph on the "ambitious" aspect of your brother, with supporting statements and details, and another paragraph on the "sociable" character of your brother, with supporting statements and details.

The following are some questions to think about as you write your draft:

- What kind of supporting details do I need?
- How many supporting details do I have to give and how long should the descriptions of them be?
- How do I avoid overlapping supporting details?

As you are writing your first draft, keep these questions in mind and check and change sentences that do not support the main idea clearly.

Revising

After the first draft, plan to revise your draft at least once. Revising means changing the organization or content of the essay and also editing the sentences.

The questions on the checklist below will help you to see if your essay is focused and well developed. You may wish to ask another person (a classmate) to comment on your essay using the checklist.

Revision Checklist

Thesis Statement	_____ Does the thesis statement state the writer's main idea adequately?
	_____ Does the thesis statement show the writer's approach or attitude toward the main idea?
Unity	_____ Do the supporting ideas show the writer's attitude toward the main idea?
	_____ Do the supporting details and examples show the writer's attitude toward the main idea?
Development	_____ Is enough evidence provided to support the main idea?
	_____ Are there sufficient supporting details?
	_____ Is the evidence that is provided convincing?
Coherence	_____ Are all the paragraphs logically connected to each other?
	_____ Do the sentences flow logically one after the other?
	_____ Are there sufficient transitions to make the sentences clear?
Purpose	_____ Is the writer's purpose clear?
	_____ Did the writer achieve what he or she wanted to convey to the reader?

Editing

Editing means checking your essay to see if you have expressed your ideas clearly and followed the rules of grammar, spelling, and punctuation.

When editing, focus on one sentence at a time. Make sure your sentences are clear and grammatically correct. Mark them for fragments or run-ons. If you are unsure about a grammatical form, consult a grammar book. When you think you may have misspelled a word, consult a dictionary.

The following is an editing checklist. The symbols on the left may be used by your instructor to indicate problem areas in your writing.

Symbol	Explanation
cap	Capital letter
lc	Lowercase (word or words incorrectly capitalized)
p	Punctuation incorrect or missing
sp	Spelling mistake
sv	Mistake in agreement of subject and verb
^	Omission (you have left something out)
frag	Sentence fragment (correct by completing sentence)
ro	Run-on sentence (insert period and capital letter or add comma and conjunction)
vt	Incorrect verb tense
vf	Verb incorrectly formed
modal	Incorrect use or formation of modal
cond	Incorrect use or formation of a conditional sentence
ss	Incorrect sentence structure
wo	Incorrect or awkward word order
conn	Incorrect or missing connector
pass	Incorrect formation or use of passive voice
unclear	Unclear message
art	Incorrect or missing article
num	Problem with the singular or plural of a noun
wc	Wrong word choice, including prepositions
wf	Wrong word form
nonidiom	Nonidiomatic (not expressed this way in English)
coh	Coherence—one idea does not lead to the next
pro re	Pronoun reference unclear or incorrect
pro agree	Pronoun agreement unclear or incorrect
¶	Begin a new paragraph here (indent)

How to Quote

In academic writing, you are expected to support your ideas to make them convincing to the reader. Writing about your own experience alone will not often convince people. If you can refer to a newspaper story, magazine article, or book in which an authority agrees with you, your ideas will have more weight.

The best way to use quoted material is to integrate it into your own writing. You should begin by saying something about the subject in your own words and then use the quotation to explain the significance of your statement.

Example:

> One aspect of the change in the nature of American society in the 1970s and the 1980s is the change in the pattern of immigration. In his book *The Unfinished Nation,* Brinkley reports, "The nation's immigration quotas expanded significantly in those years, allowing more newcomers to enter the United States legally than at any other point since the beginning of the twentieth century" (898).

The rules for quoting are as follows:

1. Put a comma after the introductory, or *reporting,* phrase and put quotation marks before and after the words quoted. Capitalize the first word of the quotation if it is the start of a sentence in the original material.

   Example:

   > He states, "In the 1970s, more than 4 million legal immigrants entered the United States."

2. If the quotation is broken, put quotation marks around both parts and separate the parts with commas. Do not begin the second part with a capital letter unless it is a new sentence.

   Example:

   > "In the 1970s," he states, "more than 4 million legal immigrants entered the United States."

Omitting Words and Adding Words

It is important to use the exact words of the author you are quoting. If you have to omit part of a quotation to fit the context of your writing, use an ellipsis, which is three spaced periods (. . .).

Example:

Brinkley states, ". . . the wave of immigration in the twenty years after 1970 was the largest of the twentieth century" (*The Unfinished Nation,* p. 898).

If you need to add words to the original quotation in order to explain it or to make it fit into the structure of your writing, put square brackets [ ] around the words you've added.

Example:

"Many Asian immigrants [Koreans, Chinese, Japanese, Indian, Filipino, Vietnamese, Thai] were highly educated professionals seeking greater opportunity in the United States," Brinkley stated.

Reporting Words

To introduce a quotation, reporting phrases such as the ones below are used:

As Brinkley said, "_____."
As he stated, "_____."
As he reported, "_____."
As he wrote, "_____."
As he declared, "_____."
As he maintained, "_____."
As he insisted, "_____."

Other reporting phrases without the word *as* can be used in the present or past tense.

Mr. Brinkley said, "_____."
He believes, "_____."
He further stated, "_____."
He continued, "_____."

Examples:

Mr. Brinkley further stated, "Already by the end of the 1980s, people of white European background constituted under 80 percent of the population (as opposed to 90 percent a half-century before)."

"It seemed likely that by the middle of the twenty-first century, he continued, "whites of European heritage would constitute less than 50 percent of the population."

Use the phrase *according to . . .* only when you are paraphrasing. Do not use *according to . . .* when citing with quotation marks.

Example:

According to the 1980 Census, 60 percent of Americans identified themselves as having English, German, or Irish ethnic origins.

or

Sixty percent of Americans identified themselves as having English, German, or Irish ethnic origins, according to the 1980 Census.

Remember *always* to document the source of your quotation, even when it is not a direct quotation.

Note on Plagiarism

Plagiarism is using other people's words or ideas without acknowledging the source of that information. You *must* use quotation marks and cite your source when you use someone's exact words. You *must* cite your source when you paraphrase. It is wrong to use another person's work without giving credit; if you do this in an assignment or on an examination, you may be disqualified from receiving a grade.

How to Paraphrase

Paraphrasing and summarizing are useful alternatives to directly quoting material from books, magazines, and other sources.

When you paraphrase, you put information from another author in different words, or rephrase it, without changing the meaning of the original. When you paraphrase, it is important to use your own words. A paraphrase should usually be the same length as the original passage so that it includes all the information.

Although you are using your own words when you paraphrase, you are expressing another author's ideas. Therefore, you must be sure to give the author credit for them; otherwise, you will be plagiarizing. Begin your paraphrase with a reference to the author and/or title of the work or the source of the article. Use phrases such as

According to [author's name], . . .
Based on [author's name]'s article in [source], . . .
In [his/her] book [title], [author's name] indicates that . . .

The following is an example of paraphrasing:

Ancient Medicine

Original:

Medicinal practices in the ancient world *were as related to* religion and philosophy as they were to science. The Egyptians were *proficient* surgeons who *employed* an *array of medications* and surgical *practices*. Their *extensive expertise involving* the human anatomy was *derived mainly from* their *practice of embalming. The ideology behind this* was that the *deceased* person's spirit, or Ka, would *perish* if the body *decomposed. To furnish an eternal abode* for the spirit, the body was *meticulously preserved.* In *another part of the ancient world,* Chinese medicine *was also linked to ideology, in particular the belief* that people are *closely linked to* a universe *dominated* by two *opposing* types of forces known as *yin* and *yang,* the negative and the positive. Physicians *were part philosophers who believed* that the harmony of the universe and the health of people depended on keeping a balance between the two forces. (*Discovery,* Everett, Reid, and Fara)

Paraphrase:

In their book *Discovery*, Everett, Reid, and Fara indicate that the practice of healing in the ancient world had as much to do with religion and philosophy as it did with science. Extremely skillful surgeons, the Egyptians used a variety of drugs and surgical techniques. Their broad knowledge of the human anatomy was primarily due to their preservation of the dead. Their belief was that the dead person's spirit, or Ka, would die if the body rotted away. In order to provide a lasting home for the spirit, the body was mummified as carefully as possible. In the ancient Far East, Chinese medicine also involved philosophical beliefs, especially the idea that people are part of a universe controlled by two conflicting forces known as *yin* and *yang*, the negative and the positive. Physicians endorsed the philosophical belief that the harmony of the universe and the health of people depended on keeping a balance between the two forces.

These are the substitutions for the italicized words in the original:

Original	Paraphrase
Medicinal practices	the practice of healing
were as related to	had as much to do with
proficient	extremely skillful
employed	used
array of medications	variety of drugs
practices	techniques
extensive expertise involving	broad knowledge of
derived mainly from	was primarily due to
practice of embalming	preservation of the dead
The ideology behind this	Their belief was
deceased	dead
perish	die
decomposed	rotted away
To furnish an eternal abode	to provide a lasting home
meticulously preserved	mummified as carefully as possible

Original	Paraphrase
another part of the ancient world	ancient Far East
was also linked to ideology	also involved philosophical beliefs
in particular the belief	especially the idea
closely linked to	depended on
dominated	controlled
opposing	conflicting
were part philosophers who believed	endorsed the philosophical belief

Some words in the original text cannot be changed because there are no synonyms for them, such as the names of people, countries, religions, and scientific terms. In this passage, for example, there are no synonyms for *Egyptians, science, Ka, Chinese, yin,* and *yang.* Not every word has to be changed in a paraphrase; a few of the original words may be kept to maintain the accuracy of a piece. In this passage, for example, important words like *ancient, religion, science, philosophy, anatomy, spirit, negative, positive, harmony,* and *universe* have not been changed.

The following are useful steps to follow when paraphrasing:

Paraphrasing Checklist

1. Read the section of the book or article over several times until you fully understand it.
2. Underline any words you do not understand. Look them up in a dictionary or use a thesaurus to find a good synonym.
3. Begin your paraphrase with a reference to the author and/or title of the book or article.
4. Rewrite each sentence, simplifying the structure and using synonyms. Rewrite each sentence one after the other.
5. Review your paraphrase. Make sure it sounds natural and like your own writing. Check to see that you have included all the information in the original and that the meaning has not been changed in any way.

Working with a partner, in a group, or on your own, paraphrase the following selections. Use a dictionary or thesaurus to find synonyms. Follow the steps listed above.

1. Although many women throughout history have been involved in the development of science, their work has gained little recognition. For a number of reasons their achievements have been ignored and their names left out of books. (Everett, Reid, and Fara, *Discovery*, p. 92)

2. Observe a group of listeners the next time a good storyteller tells an obscene joke. Skilled joke tellers elaborate on details. They allow the tension to build gradually as they set up the punch line. Listeners smile or blush slightly as the joke progresses. According to Freud, this long building creates greater tension and thus a louder and longer laugh when the punch line finally allows a tension release. (Burger, *Personality*, p. 99)

3. Three decades of research has demonstrated that people exposed to aggressive models sometimes imitate the aggressive behavior. This finding holds true for children as well as adults. But clearly, simple exposure to an aggressive model is not enough to turn us into violent people. Anyone who has watched television or attended a few movies recently undoubtedly has seen some murders, beatings, shootings, and the like. Yet rarely do we leave the theatre in search of victims. (Burger, *Personality*, p. 445)

How to Summarize

A summary is very similar to a paraphrase, only shorter. When you summarize, you put published information in your own words and include all the important information, without changing its meaning, just as you do when you paraphrase. However, when you summarize, you reduce the amount of information. The length of summaries varies. For example, the summary of a book may be several pages long, while the summary of an article may be one paragraph.

In a summary, only the main ideas and key points are stated, and repetitions of the same idea are left out. Since you include only the main ideas in a summary, it is helpful to make a brief outline before you begin to summarize.

The following is an example of a paraphrase, outline, and summary.

Personality Types

Original:

What kind of people are likely candidates for heart attacks and what kind are not? Typical Type A people are the most susceptible to heart problems because they are strongly motivated to overcome obstacles and are driven to achieve and to meet goals. They are attracted to competition, enjoy power and recognition, and are easily aroused to anger and action. They dislike wasting time and do things in a vigorous and efficient manner. On the other hand, Type B people are relaxed and unhurried. They may work hard on occasion, but rarely in the driven, compulsive manner of Type A people. These people are less likely than Type A's to seek the stress of competition or to be aroused to anger or action. Naturally not all people classified as Type A or Type B fit these profiles exactly, and there are times when Type A people behave in a Type B manner and vice versa. But, as with other traits, researchers can identify the extent to which each of us behaves, on the average, and assign us a personality type on the basis of which some startling predictions can be made. (*Personality,* Burger)

Paraphrase:

Which personalities are prone to heart attacks and which are not? According to Burger in his book *Personality,* classic Type A people are most at risk for coronary problems because of their intense desire to conquer barriers and their drive to realize their goals. They like competition, relish power and recognition, have quick tempers, and are readily provoked to action. Time is of the essence, so they do things energetically and efficiently. On the other hand, Type B people are calm and unhurried. Periodically, they may work hard, but hardly ever in the compelling, compulsive way of Type A people. Type B's are less likely than Type A's to be competitive or to be incited to anger or action. Of course, not all people identified as Type A or Type B conform to these profiles exactly. Occasionally, Type A people exhibit Type B characteristics and vice versa. But, as with other traits, researchers can determine the measure of our average behavior and attribute a personality type to us, which can tell some very surprising things about us.

Outline:
A. Type A people
   1. At risk for heart attacks
   2. Driven, competitive, quick-tempered, time-conscious, energetic, and efficient
B. Type B people
   1. Calm and unhurried
   2. Less competitive and slower to react
C. On the basis of average behavior, people can be categorized according to well-defined personality types.

Summary:

According to Burger in his book *Personality,* people can be categorized into well-defined personality types on the basis of their average behavior. Type A people tend to be more at risk for heart attacks because they are driven, competitive, quick-tempered, time-conscious, energetic, and efficient. Type B people, on the other hand, are calm, unhurried, less competitive, and less reactive than their Type A counterparts.

You can see from the outline that the main idea (item C) is stated in the last sentence of the passage. In your summary, however, you write the main idea first and then add one sentence for each of the two supporting ideas (items A and B).

Summary Checklist

1. Begin with a reference to the author and/or title of the book or article. Include the source of the article.
2. Identify and write the main ideas and key points.
3. Do not include details or repeat ideas.

Exercise 2

Summarize the following passages in a few sentences. Check your work against the summary checklist.

1. Music video is a relatively new entry into the world of television, having become common only in the 1980s. Music video is difficult to categorize and to illustrate with one example, because it includes so many different types of expression. The definitive characteristic is in its name: There is music and there is video imagery. Some music videos dramatize the words of a song or even create brief visual dramas that are only vaguely related to the music. Some offer a message or statement. Some are relatively straightforward recordings of the performers at work. Obviously, defining the art of music video is not an easy task. (*Living with Art,* Rita Gilbert)

2. Charles Darwin, an English naturalist and explorer, began a five-year expedition in December 1831 on a ship called the *Beagle.* The expedition reached Bahia in Brazil in the spring of 1832. Darwin was amazed by the number and dazzling colors of the flowers and birds he saw. The *Beagle* then sailed south along the coast of Patagonia where the crew discovered the fossil remains of several extinct animals. In September 1835 the expedition reached the remote Galapagos Islands. There Darwin saw birds, animals and plants that are found nowhere else on earth because they had developed in isolation from their relatives in America. They were to play an important part in Darwin's theories on how animals and humans evolved. (*Discovery,* Everett, Reid, and Fara)

3. Beginning in the Middle East at least 10,000 years ago, some peoples began to purposely sow the seeds of their food plants. It was a practice that allowed them to produce adequate amounts of food in the areas near their settlements rather than pursuing game and living as nomads. At the same time, they gradually tamed and domesticated wild animals for their food, hides and labor. An agricultural lifestyle led to the first towns and cities, the development of tools, baskets and pots, which led to the development of commerce and new crafts and skills. Agriculture played a significant role in developing the control over our existence that distinguishes humans from other species. (*Biology!*, Postlethwait, Hopson, and Veres)

Answer Key

Chapter 1: Artists (page 2)
1. Georgia O'Keeffe   2. Claude Monet   3. Vincent van Gogh
4. Salvador Dali   5. Paul Gauguin

Chapter 2: Language (page 34)
1. a. Correct   b. bachelor   c. superintendent   d. excerpt
   e. Correct   f. tariff   g. occurrence   h. newsstand   i. Correct
   j. Correct
2. colour, center, behavior, theatre, gaol, judgment, programme, skillful, cheque, draught

Chapter 3: Hygiene (page 63)
1. False   2. True   3. True   4. False   5. True   6. False

Chapter 4: Groups, Organizations, and Societies (page 92)
1. Scouts   2. The Amish   3. Greenpeace   4. Salvation Army
5. Masons

Chapter 7: Nutrition (page 179)
1. Bread   2. Ham   3. Margarine   4. Mayonnaise

(continued from page ii)

Skills Index